Twayne's United States Authors Series

Sylvia E. Bowman, *Editor*

INDIANA UNIVERSITY

Wallace Stevens

(TUSAS) 127

WALLACE STEVENS

By WILLIAM BURNEY
Central Connecticut State College

TWAYNE PUBLISHERS

A DIVISION OF G. K. HALL & CO., BOSTON

Library of Congress Catalog Card Number: 67-28857

ISBN 0-8057-0696-8

MANUFACTURED IN THE UNITED STATES OF AMERICA

To the Memory of
Martha Gearhart Burney

Contents

About the Author

William Burney is currently with the Department of English at Central Connecticut State College, where he teaches courses on the poetry of Pound, Eliot, Yeats, and Stevens, and on the modern novel. Burney has also taught at Michigan State University. His study of Wallace Stevens is the culmination of intensive research on the poet which he began in 1957.

Preface

THIS STUDY of Wallace Stevens is largely an exercise in paraphrase, but it also assumes that the reader has read the poems. Stevens' central problem, which remained the same throughout his poetic career, was the characteristic modern epistemological problem: what is real? But Stevens' approach to the problem necessarily changed as he grew older and more experienced as a poet and as a man. What I have tried to do in this study is to point out the aspect of this problem that interested or troubled him during each period of his life. I have concentrated almost entirely on *The Collected Poems* because it seems to me that Stevens put those poems into an order that was intended to emphasize the changes in his approach. Any poem by Stevens can be related to any other of his poems; a reader of this book can find in each poem that I treat countless aspects that I do not touch, simply by comparing it with poems other than the ones with which I have compared it. All I have done is to compare the import of each poem with that of those poems among which Stevens has purposely placed it. Only in my treatment of the poems in *Harmonium* have I discussed the poems in a sequence other than the one in which Stevens chose to place them.

Since this study is in part an effort to lay bare the elementary patterns of Stevens' intellectual intentions, it may seem premature because no biography of the poet has yet been published. There is the bare chronology of birth, education, employment, publication, and death, which has been well known for a long time; and there are the obvious topical references in the poems to the Great Depression, to World War II and to other events. And now there are the letters collected by Holly Stevens which unfortunately appeared after this essay was finished. I have not attempted a biographical sketch because it would be of no more use than the bare chronology. But I believe that an exercise in paraphrase is not premature; it is one of the necessary starting points for criticism. And in the form which I have attempted here, it is a preliminary sketch of Stevens' intellectual autobiography. I have limited myself to descriptive generalizations based on the content and tone of the poems or on common experiences, like those of the Great Depression and World War II. For the same reason, I have made, at the end of this study, only a few suggestions about Stevens' place in the literary and philosophical traditions.

But some readers, especially experts on Stevens, may ask, why paraphrase? Isn't that rather too humble a goal? This study is addressed primarily to the general reader, not to the expert on Stevens, or even to the expert on poetry. And it is my experience that college students, for instance, have difficulty with Stevens on this most elementary level: just what is he saying? Most people respond immediately and positively to Stevens' elegance of language, his fantastic exactitude of imagery, even to his subtle probing for the rhythms of meditation. But most people, probably because it was Stevens' intention, are constantly at sea in his poems, constantly wondering where they are going now, and why.

Not that this study is a road map, with fixed lines and clearly named stopping places. It is more like a series of weather maps, with arrows indicating the directions of the winds. The general movement of the weather of Stevens' *mundo* can be stated fairly simply; but, by the same token, such deeply significant shifts in attitude as that from transmogrified hymns to the Virgin in *Harmonium* to guilty and fearful attacks on the earthly mother in the later poems must be left to speak for themselves.

WILLIAM BURNEY

Acknowledgments

I am grateful to the Estate of Wallace Stevens and to Alfred A. Knopf, Inc., the publisher of Wallace Stevens, for permitting me to reprint from the following copyrighted editions: *The Necessary Angel* (1951), *The Collected Poems of Wallace Stevens* (1954), and *Opus Posthumous* (1957). I am also grateful to Charles Scribner's Sons for permitting me to reprint from George Santayana's *The Sense of Beauty* (1896) and his *Interpretations of Poetry and Religion* (1900).

Finally, I am most grateful to Professor Sylvia Bowman and Mr. William S. Osborne for their skillful and conscientious editing of the manuscript, and to Holly Stevens for supplying me with some genealogical details.

Chronology

1879 October 2, Wallace Stevens born in Reading, Pennsylvania.

1897- Harvard undergraduate, enrolled as a special student.
1900

1900- Reporter for *New York Herald Tribune.*
1901

1901 Entered New York Law School.

1904 Admitted to New York State bar.

1909 Married Elsie V. Kachel.

1911 Stevens' father died.

1912 Mother died.

1914 First publication of Stevens' mature work, in September issue of *The Trend,* and, more significantly, in November issue of *Poetry: A Magazine of Verse.*

1916 Joined legal staff of Hartford Accident and Indemnity Company.

1923 *Harmonium.*

1934 Became vice-president of Hartford Accident and Indemnity Company.

1936 *Ideas of Order.*

1937 *The Man with the Blue Guitar.*

1942 *Parts of a World.*

1946 Became a member of the National Institute of Arts and Letters.

1947 *Transport to Summer.*

1950 *The Auroras of Autumn.* Awarded Bollingen Prize in Poetry.

1951 *The Necessary Angel: Essays on Reality and the Imagination.*

1954 *The Collected Poems of Wallace Stevens.*

1955 Awarded Pulitzer Prize for poetry and National Book Award. August 2, Wallace Stevens died.

1957 *Opus Posthumous.*

Wallace Stevens

CHAPTER 1

The Plays and *Harmonium*

I *The Plays*

W ALLACE STEVENS' PLAYS serve as an excellent intro-
duction to his works because they contain some of the
least obscure poetry of his early period and because their explicit-
ness provides a convenient introduction to a central quality of
his imagination: the histrionic. His imagination is more theatrical
than dramatic, as Stevens himself admitted in one of his *Adagia*:
"Life is an affair of people not of places. But for me life is an
affair of places and that is the trouble." *Three Travellers Watch
a Sunrise*—a play which was published in 1916 (two years after
Stevens began to publish poems) is Stevens' most complete ar-
rangement of the personae of his poetic *mundo*. The three
Chinese personify the three aspects of his style and his poetic
attitude; the Negroes, the blackness of reality against which his
imagination fought; the girl and the man, the vulgar personal life
of the world that interferes with a clear and simple confrontation
between imagination and reality.

The First Chinese clothes himself in red; he is the first to no-
tice the creaking of the limb; he thirsts for real water, from a
melon or a spring, and he pooh-poohs the Second and the Third
Chinese' talk of beauty and poetry and the satisfactions of per-
ception. The First Chinese is the red-blooded man, the part of
the poet that responds unthinkingly and insensitively to elemental
needs. He sings a somewhat cynical song of Mistress and Maid
and makes up a ballad, which turns out to be true, about the
man who has gone away with his neighbor's daughter.

The Second Chinese clothes himself in blue; when the First
calls his attention to the creaking limb he says, "It is only a tree/
Creaking in the night wind." When the First sees the girl, he
drops his stringed instrument, but the Second approaches her

and speaks to her. The Second is "a man of sense and sympathy" who reads from a book and insists on the need for "the invasion of humanity," and the poverty and wretchedness which that invasion causes, in order that there be love and wisdom. The Second speaks for Stevens' tendency to be didactic, reasonable, and intent on principles and maxims.

The Third Chinese clothes himself in green; about the creaking limb he says, "There would be no creaking/In the windless pavilions." He wants to believe that the candle or the sun can shine in seclusion "for the beauty of shining." He speaks the final words in the play, expressing an acceptance of the color red as the color of blood, of a dead man's eyes, of a grieving girl's eyes, and of the sun. And in accepting this red resemblance between these very various things, he also embraces multiple points of view, because "Sunrise is multiplied,/Like the earth on which it shines,/By the eyes that open on it." The Third Chinese speaks for the all-embracing power of metaphor, which was for Stevens the end and consummation of the poetic process. The First Chinese represents the brute beginning of the process; and the Second, the rational or philosophic way to the end.

The Negroes represent the starkest anti-poetic. The Negro remaining on the stage after all the other living characters have left is the blackness that the dead man's eyes see. When the remaining Negro strikes the instrument, "One or two birds twitter" (birds, in Stevens' poetry, tend to speak for insensate reality, "mind without any dream" [*Collected Poems*, 394]), "A voice, urging a horse, is heard at a distance. There is the crack of a whip." (This is an early version of "the giant sense, the enormous harnesses/And writhing wheels of this world's business,/The drivers in the wind-blows cracking whips" [*CP* 308]). The Negroes, then, represent a form of unconscious being which is at one with the elemental forces of things; they are black, unspeaking, practical; they are servants, and yet they are a form of being which precedes our conscious being (the Negroes appear on stage before the Chinese) and which will remain after the reader has gone.

The man and the girl provide the three Chinese with a subject for conversation and song, rather amusing or rather disturbing, according to the lights of each Chinese. The plight of the girl takes the First and the Second Chinese away from the scene of their meditations and their banter. Only the Third is detached enough to achieve a final integration of all the elements in the scene. Only metaphor can embrace all the goods and evils of life and death.

Stevens' poetry abounds with "he's" and "she's" that are defined as persons only by their ways of seeing the world. They are simply points of view. *Three Travellers* is a conveniently explicit introduction to this method, but *Carlos among the Candles* carries the reader one step deeper into the method in its more implicit form. Carlos is dressed in black, but carries a white candle. He is thus from the outset a figure that combines the unconsciouness of the Negroes with the metaphorical super-consciousness of the Third Chinese. The action of *Carlos among the Candles* is simply the creation and decreation of a day, or a year, by the lighting and then by the blowing out, one by one, of twenty-four candles. At the end Carlos blows out his white candle and leaps out the window into the night, crying, "Oh, ho! Here is matter beyond invention." His creative and destructive action has nerved him, "an eccentric pedant of about forty," to leap into his own primitive unconsciousness, his sleep or his death. In the creative-destructive process he has embraced all possible points of view, peopled and unpeopled his world, and so has shown himself that he need have no more fear of nothingness than, say, God has.

Crispin, the hero of Stevens' first long poem, "The Comedian as the Letter C," is a figure much like Carlos. He too creates and uncreates his world; and he also comes in the end to accept death as nothingness. In the process, he passes through a more densely furnished world; and Stevens apparently intended his progress to integrate the themes of his first book of poems, *Harmonium.* As an integration it is more a melody than a chord, and it has to be studied more closely than *Carlos among the Candles* to see the relation of the parts to one another and to the whole which they form.

II   *"The Comedian as the Letter C"*

In "The Comedian as the Letter C" there are three central themes under which one can gather, in one way or another, all the poems in *Harmonium,* as well as all the rest of Stevens' available poems. The three themes are nothingness or death, life, and the vulgar; and a survey of "The Comedian" shows what these three themes mean and how they relate to one another.

The hero of the poem, Crispin, begins as an idealist, believing that "man is the intelligence of his soil,/The sovereign ghost." That attitude works splendidly in France, where Crispin has his origin. There he has "a barber's eye, an eye of land, or simple salad-beds"; but, at sea, his eye is bewildered and overwhelmed by "Inscrutable hair in an inscrutable world." Hair that will not be trimmed or kept in bounds means throughout Stevens' poetry some kind of natural and usually sexual wildness and fecundity. This ocean of too many impressions, too many words, has the effect of being sublime, virtually unnameable; and so it is called "The World Without Imagination," a world overflowing with what Stevens later called "the murderous alphabet." It doesn't quite kill Crispin, but it makes him "a starker barer self/In a starker, barer world." The "starker, barer world" is predominantly the ocean-like flux of experience. Stevens chooses to dignify it as "the veritable ding an sich"; and, indeed, throughout his poetry the thing in itself, the ultimate reality, is most of all an inscrutable and apparently chaotic motion in otherwise blank space. His last long poem, "An Ordinary Evening in New Haven," concludes

> It is not in the premise that reality
> Is a solid. It may be a shade that traverses
> A dust, a force that traverses a shade.

At the end of the first part of "The Comedian," this basic reality is called "caparison of wind and cloud." It is, in other words, a kind of nothingness with some force at large in it. Like Kant's *ding an sich*, it is ultimately God, whom Stevens in a late poem suggests ought to be "a vermilioned nothingness." Or, as he says in his "Adagia," "Reality is a vacuum."

He also says in his "Adagia," "Reality is the spirit's true center"; and this is certainly true of Crispin after crossing the ocean. In the second part of "The Comedian," "Concerning the Thunderstorms of Yucatan," Crispin is destitute; the reality that was his spirit's true center was indeed a vacuum: "He was in this as other freemen are,/Sonorous nutshells rattling inwardly." And so "His violence was for aggrandizement/And not for stupor."

As a consequence, he finds no aid in the nightingale, to whom the Maya sonneteers still make their plea. Crispin is not even aided by the bright-colored tropical birds. What finally does aid him is the thunderstorms that come from the mountains.

Out of the vacuum that is the reality at the spirit's true center —out of that utter destitution or, as he more frequently called it, poverty—there arises a violent desire for aggrandizement, for the height and weight of mountains and for the gigantic tones of thunder. The mountain is as important an image as the sea in Stevens' poetry, and this is the first clear appearance of it. As it is here, it is usually associated with the hero; and although Crispin is rather an anti-hero, at this moment in the poem he would like to be a hero. This mountain-like hero is Stevens' most central image of life at its noblest, which for the poet is the only life worthy of the name. It is the "life" already referred to as one of Stevens' three central themes.

If, as Paul Rosenfeld suggests, the thunderstorms gave "the feeling of the war"[1]—World War I—then the appearance of heroic aspirations in Crispin at this point in time directly anticipates the appearance of the fully formed hero in the poems which Stevens wrote in the early years of World War II. Certainly prominent among Stevens' first mature poems in print were "Phases," a series of war poems published in 1914; and his spirit and his poetry noticeably awakened from the demoralized feelings of the Depression when, in 1936, the Spanish Civil War began. Indeed, Stevens seemingly regarded all his poetry as a response to the condition of war: in 1942 he described the period since the crash of 1929 as "a war-like whole" (*Necessary Angel,* 21), but at some time near the beginning of the Spanish Civil War he applied the same description to the period since the beginning of World War I (*Opus Posthumous,* 224)—that is, since he had begun seriously to publish poetry.

Whether the thunderstorms of Yucatan in "The Comedian" give the feeling of the war or not, they have the same effect on Crispin: that of the sublime, which is surely what Stevens is describing when he says of the "war-like whole":

> We are confronting, therefore, a set of events, not only beyond our power to tranquilize them in the mind, beyond our power to reduce them and metamorphose them, but events that stir the emotions to violence, that engage us in what is direct and im-

mediate and real, and events that involve the concepts and sanc-
tions that are the order of our lives and may involve our very
lives. . . . (NA, 22)

To resist or evade, successfully, such a pressure of reality is, as
one has noted in Crispin, to be possessed by a new and heroic
self. And so in "Approaching Carolina," the third major division
of "The Comedian," Crispin repudiates the possibilities of poetry
presented by his childhood fantasy of America as a cold, moonlit
continent. He repudiates them because they are "lesser things/
Than the relentless contact he desires." This contact is to fill out
and liberate his self: it is to evoke in him his noblest life.

But, whereas the liberation and fulfillment which he felt in
Yucatan were sublime, the fulfillment he now seeks is what
might be called "beautiful," using a distinction that Santayana
made in *The Sense of Beauty*, which was intended as an under-
graduate text on the subject and which was first published the
year before Stevens entered Harvard, where Santayana was a
teacher. Santayana makes this distinction between the beautiful
and the sublime:

> Now it is the essential privilege of beauty to so synthesize and
> bring to a focus the various impulses of the self, so to suspend
> them to a single image, that a great peace falls upon that per-
> turbed kingdom. In the experience of these momentary harmonies
> we have the basis of the enjoyment of beauty, and of all its mys-
> tical meanings. But there are always two methods of securing
> harmony: one is to unify all the given elements, and another is to
> reject and expunge all the elements that refuse to be unified.
> Unity by inclusion gives us the beautiful; unity by exclusion, op-
> position, and isolation gives us the sublime. Both are pleasures:
> but the pleasure of the one is warm, passive, and pervasive; that
> of the other cold, imperious, and keen. The one identifies us with
> the world, the other raises us above it.[2]

Crispin's pleasure was "cold, imperious, and keen" when his mind
was "free/And more than free, elate, intent, profound/And
studious of a self possessing him," when he heard the thunder
in Yucatan. And "to reject and expunge all the elements that
refuse to be unified" is to resist or evade, successfully, "a set of
events . . . beyond our power to tranquilize them in the mind,
beyond our power to reduce them and metamorphose them." By
contrast, in approaching Carolina

> It was a flourishing tropic he required
> For his refreshment, an abundant zone,
> Prickly and obdurate, dense, harmonious,
> Yet with a harmony not rarified
> Nor fined for the inhibited instruments
> Of over-civil stops.

Here is the "unity by inclusion" that gives a "warm, passive, and pervasive" pleasure and which "identifies us with the world." In Carolina this means identity with all things, including "the vulgar," which Crispin claims as "his theme" and which is vividly brought home to him when he arrives there. He comes as a hero, ideally in search of "the fecund minimum," the possibility of life where it would seem impossible (that is, for instance, in the presence of the thunderstorms in Yucatan). But now the better part of valor seems to be an all-accepting esthetic, a search for beauty in the rankest scene imaginable.

To accept the world so thoroughly is, as Santayana says, to identify oneself with it; hence "The Idea of a Colony," the next major division of "The Comedian," begins with "Nota: his soil is man's intelligence." Crispin is now at the opposite pole from his position at the beginning of the poem, which was, "Nota: man is the intelligence of his soil,/The sovereign ghost." But his submission to the intelligence of the American soil soon leads him to imagine everyone in the Western hemisphere doing likewise: he would be a kind of poetic father of his hemisphere, a master colonizer who would set the supreme example of serving "Grotesque apprenticeship to chance event,/A clown, perhaps, but an aspiring clown."

He is also a religious leader. It is important to notice that in detail the poetry expected to come from the pan-American "clerks of our experience" has a deliberately liturgical sound:

> The melon should have apposite ritual,
> Performed in verd apparel, and the peach,
> When its black branches came to bud, belle day,
> Should have an incantation. And again,
> When piled on salvers its aroma steeped
> The summer, it should have a sacrament
> And celebration.

The reader may remember that, during the thunderstorms in Yucatan, Crispin knelt in the cathedral with the rest: as a "connoisseur of elemental fate," he was "aware of exquisite thought." Stevens finds some reason to speak from within a cathedral in two other important long poems—"The Man with the Blue Guitar" and "Notes Toward a Supreme Fiction"—and in *Harmonium* there are several transmogrified hymns or litanies to the Virgin. Transmogrified liturgy is, of course, nothing unusual in a modern poet, especially one in the tradition of Baudelaire; nor is it unexpected that Stevens says in his Adagia that "Poetry is a means of redemption."

In planning his "polar planterdom," Crispin completely throws out his "mental moonlight"—his juvenile dreams of America as cold and moonlit. Apparently, he has not repudiated it completely; indeed, the preceding section says that he regularly vacillated between sun and moon, even though his response to the moon was to deny himself many of the poems it inspired. However, his colonizing project soon appeared to be objectionable for the same reason that the moonlit fiction was:

> These bland excursions into time to come,
> Related in romance to backward flights,
> However prodigal, however proud,
> Contained in their afflatus the reproach
> That first drove Crispin to his wandering.

The moonlight fiction of his youth and the kitchen-garden idealism with which he began in France are both of a piece with his colonizing project, and the inevitable reaction against them occurs at the beginning of Part V, "A Nice Shady Home." Crispin gives up his heroic aspirations when he stops before a plum, which is "good, fat, guzzly fruit" no matter what is said or thought about it.

The quotidian plum stops him, and, further, "The plum survives its poems." The plum satisfies him, but it is not his creature: it has a permanent existence of its own. "So Crispin hasped on the surviving form,/For him, of shall or ought to be in is."

This is a comic reduction, but Crispin is giving up heroic and therefore tragic projects because he cannot imagine laying by the personal and making of his own fate "an instance of all fate." In spite of this apparently extreme repudiation of all pretentions, he is back where he began, in a kitchen-garden variety of ideal-ism: "The very man despising honest quilts/Lies quilted to his poll in his despite./For realist, what is is what should be." This line recalls the lines at the beginning of the poem: "An eye of land, of simple salad-beds,/Of honest quilts, the eye of Crispin. . . ." What has happened is that, by the act of reducing *what ought to be* to *what is, what is* becomes *what ought to be.* In his later terminology, when the real supplants the unreal, the real becomes itself unreal. If value is made into fact, then fact be-comes value.

But there is a difference; for, before he set out on his voyage, Crispin was a foppish valet. Probably his name comes from Le Sage's *Crispin rival de son maitre,* though in "Anecdote of the Abnormal" (*OP,* 23), a poem written three or four years before "The Comedian," Stevens addresses a persona much like the Crispin of the later poem as "Crispin-valet, Crispin-saint!" Saint Crispin and his brother Crispinian were reputedly Roman nobles who gave up their property and went to what is now France to be missionaries, supporting themselves by shoemaking, which could be regarded as a valet-like service.

What is more to the point, however, is the westward move-ment of both Saint Crispin and the Crispin of "The Comedian" to what was a colony, so that Crispin becomes saintly when he gives up his idealistic "property" in France and here in "A Nice Shady Home" appears as a "hermit, pure and capable." A fop in France, he is a hermit in Carolina. But as the hermit becomes less discontented, more cosseted by the good, guzzly quotidian plum, he becomes quite the opposite of a saint. He becomes a pioneer planter, marries his "prismy blond," and lives

> Like Candide,
> Yeoman and grub, but with a fig in sight,
> And cream for the fig and silver for the cream,
> A blonde to tip the silver and to taste
> The rapey gouts.

This quotidian saps him, even as a searcher for the truth; but it also gives a humped return: "Daughters with Curls," the subject of the sixth and last major division of the poem.

Crispin's daughters are surely the seasons, as Frank Kermode insists,[3] and they thereby represent another way in which Crispin

rounds out his esthetic: their perpetual recurrence and their
coming to full development act for his life as a

> summary,
> Autumn's compendium, strident in itself
> But muted, mused, and perfectly revolved
> In those portentous accents, syllables,
> And sounds of music coming to accord
> Upon his lap, like their inherent sphere.

The daughter seasons thus composed Crispin's endlessly turning
mundo, and yet "The Comedian" concludes with an oddly fatal-
istic shrug. It says, in effect, that, if this *mundo* turns out to be
false, then fortunately the poet sooner or later must die. "So may
the relation of each man be clipped." This statement, I think,
accounts for the title: the letter "C" is the eternal circle of the
seasons clipped by death. The poem which Stevens placed after
"The Comedian"—"From the Misery of Don Joost"—confirms this
interpretation: "The senses and feeling, the very sound/And
sight, and all there was of the storm,/knows nothing more." In
his later poems this circle is more often eccentric, as contrasted
with concentric; but, as an eccentric circle, life goes on. In "The
Comedian" the clipped circle is simply a dead end.

The end of the poem, then, represents a different kind of
death or nothingness than did the ocean at the beginning or the
thunderstorms in the second part. The earlier purgative and
sublime experiences left him discontented and elated; they pro-
duced in him a heroic self, a self whose poetical projects were
hemispheric in scope and who at least aspired to be noble. The
experience of death anticipated at the end is the vulgar end of a
vulgar life, a consolation with the quality of self-indulgent fatal-
ism that had "Confined . . . cosseted" and "condoned" him so that
he gradually gave up his heroic aspirations and embraced, with
hedonistic gusto, an ordinary life full of sensual pleasures.

There is no reason why a vulgar life should not end vulgarly,
but Crispin—and Stevens—would like to imagine another alterna-
tive: out of the vulgar life come celebrations of the seasons that
are such that the seasons so celebrated continue to revolve for-
ever. But the insistence that the poet's life be a quotidian or
vulgar one and the precautionary ending of the poem seem to
suggest that such immortal celebrations may not come out of

such contented ordinariness. The fully developed hero of the poems written early in World War II will contain both Crispin's heroic and his quotidian aspect. "Asides on the Oboe," published in 1940, emphasizes the hero's centrally representative character: he is "the man of glass,/Who in a million diamonds sums us up." (It should be remembered that Crispin refused to lay by the personal and make his fate an instance of all fate, which he would have to do in order to be a hero.) The hero in "Asides on the Oboe" is also certain of his ability to produce real seasons: he is, again, "The man of glass, cold and numbered," who "dewily cries, 'Thou art not August unless I make thee so.'" But this hero is also a man whose experience is quite ordinary. In "Examination of the Hero in a Time of War," published in 1942, "These are the works and pastimes/Of the highest self: he studies the paper/On the wall, the lemons on the table./This is his day."

In 1923, when Stevens was writing "The Comedian" in order to give the readers of *Harmonium* an idea of the order underlying his early poems, he may very well have known that he would not publish many poems in the next six years. The prospect of so much inaction may have made him wonder, quite honestly and quite understandably, what would happen to his poetic development. He was not satisfied with most of the poems he had written thus far. He believed deeply in the combination of qualities with which he endowed Crispin, the vulgar clown who has in him the possibility of being noble and heroic, who lives an ordinary sensual life, and who may yet be able to make out of it the very world that will continue to turn after he dies. But, it seems quite reasonable to suppose, Stevens could not be sure about these heroic possibilities. They had shown themselves clearly in only one poem in *Harmonium*, "Tea at the Palaz of Hoon," and there in a way that hardly looks heroic unless the poem is seen in a perspective that includes all the later hero poems. Stevens was understandably diffident, but he was also cynical. When the reader looks at his attachment to the vulgar as a theme, he will find that it is equalled by his hatred of it as a fact. The result is ambivalence, at the least, and what might at the best be called "The Weeping Burgher" predicament. Being a poet and a successful lawyer-businessman might tend to make anyone cynical.

Before discussing the vulgar, let me discuss death and life and in that order; for death is clearly the most important theme in "The Comedian": life is the natural effect of the fear of death; and the vulgar, again as it occurs in "The Comedian," is an ignoble kind of life and death with which Stevens, sometimes a little uncertainly, contrasts genuine or noble life and death.

III Death and Nothingness

It is very hard to believe that the poems in *Harmonium* were put together in an over-all pattern. It is believable that Stevens tried to find some pattern, but he virtually confesses failure when he says in "The Comedian" that "he humbly served/Grotesque apprenticeship to chance event." Nevertheless, in what must be accepted as an ocean of chance events, the reader discovers islands of order—little clumps of poems that seem to be related to one another. Two of the three central poems of death and nothingness—"Domination of Black" and "Thirteen Ways of Looking at a Blackbird"—are the first and the last really strikingly successful and important poems one encounters in the first edition of *Harmonium*. (The poems between "Nomad Exquisite" and "Tea" in *Collected Poems* were not in the first edition of *Harmonium*). The third, "The Snow Man," is placed significantly next to "Domination of Black." Stevens virtually enters and exits with a black line, as if to say that life can be celebrated only within the margins of a death notice.

"Domination of Black"—and its counterpart "Thirteen Ways of Looking at a Blackbird"—are not only poems about the black aspect of reality; they are carefully worked out exercises in the relations between perception and imagination. Crispin's experience has already indicated that this is a significant association: at the sound of thunder, his imagination towers. The perception of death or nothingness is notoriously difficult to preserve as a perception: it too quickly turns into pure emotion.

What "Domination of Black" does with visual experience is quite interesting. It expresses the inner-outer character of experience: there is a correspondence between colors inside the room and those outside. In general, when Stevens uses the image of a room with a window, he is thinking of the mind with some mode of perception, characteristically visual. In this room there is a fire (the lamp, rather than the mirror), which repeats the colors of the fallen leaves outside. Outside, darkness is coming on; and the inner-outer dichotomy creates an atmosphere of fear. The mind feels at the mercy of outer darkness—death—which, as in "From the Misery of Don Joost," brings an end to light and color. Also, the outer darkness corresponds with a darkness within the room: for the metaphor of the "the fallen leaves/Repeating themselves," indicates that the fire is the only light in the room and that it is mostly dark. Further, the lack of color—the un-named (except in the title) blackness outside—is brought to bear by the heavy hemlocks, which, standing tall and seeming darker and darker, have an encroaching, menacing quality. The fact that no color is named, except "Black" in the title, makes any abstract thought about the situation impossible.

The situation is altogether one of several *things* in resemblance and conflict with one another: the fire resembles the fallen leaves, and the two of them are in conflict with the striding hemlocks. This situation suggests that the fallen leaves, bright as they are, are already victims of death. They are not like "The big-finned palm,/And green vine angering for life" in "Nomad Exquisite" which corresponds with "Forms, flames, and the flakes of flames" that come flinging in the mind of the poet. The fire in "Domination of Black," therefore, corresponds with a dying glory of colors outside; and the fact that the color of the heavy hemlocks is not named makes it as formidable as unnamed gods traditionally are. Abstract thought is a form of incantatory magic; once a quality is named, it is domesticated; it can be commanded to come or go, sit or lie, like a dog.

The absence of abstract thought, on the other hand, leaves one in a condition of awe and contrition. All one can do to meet an unnamed quality is to find within oneself something equally unnamed but more vivid as a countervailing violence; and in this poem, fear brings to memory the cry of the peacocks. That fear brought the cry to memory, or that the cry corresponds with the sound of the fire, is not yet evident to the speaker. All he knows is the association, but it has an emotionally impelling quality that makes the speaker remember seeing resemblances between the colors of the peacocks' tails and those of the leaves and of the fire. His reliving these correspondences (in the second section the time is twilight, rather than night) sets up a hypnotically revolving figure out of which there finally emerges, as if from a trance, the correspondence that originally evoked the cry of the peacocks: the sound of the fire. But, in the process, there is added to the ambiguity of whether the cry is against the twilight or against the leaves (which, because they resemble the peacock tails are *rivals* in color and in feeling) the possibility that the peacocks have carried the fight into the enemy's camp and are attacking the very hemlocks themselves.

More important than any clear decision about who is on what side and who is winning is the fact that the conflict has been entirely externalized. The cry of the peacocks begins as a memory; but, as the peacocks become visually vivid and part of the scene, the cry becomes immediately audible: "I heard them cry." The remembered fight is going on outside. The poet's champion, the peacocks, have gone outside to meet the black; the speaker therefore feels safer and looks out the window at the night sky. Up to this time he has barely left the fire and perhaps has hardly looked away from it. And now, for the first time, he self-consciously reports a perception: "I saw how the planets gathered." But no sooner is he timidly meeting the world with his glass-protected eye than what meets his eye suggests the same round of fearful images—the leaves, the wind, the night, the hemlocks. He has not left the room, with its self-conscious self-reference (I heard, I saw, I saw), and so, finally, the cry of the peacocks can only be a *memory* and no help (he can't *hear* them anymore) for the self-conscious fear (I *felt* afraid) he feels when confronting the conflict, now cosmic in its proportions, between the dominant black and the gathering planets, which are just as doomed to blackness as the leaves.

Although at the end he is able to admit that he felt afraid (when Stevens uses the pronoun "I" he usually intends to imply a reflective or introspective movement of consciousness), and thus is able to name his emotion, he is not able to domesticate it; he is still unable to name the external threat, and he is himself more a victim of his own domestication, his having to remain behind a window, in a room, in a house. All he can do is remember the cry of the peacocks; and, since they were unable to hold the hemlocks at bay on the first encounter (if, indeed, they were on the speaker's side), they are not likely to be much help on the second.

The import of the poem is that there is something about the

absence of light, and therefore the absence of color, that the mind cannot name, and therefore cannot tame. As a negation—a lack of light and color—and as an unintelligible quality, unnamed and untamed, this dominant black is an excellent example of what Stevens means by saying that "Reality is a vacuum." Not only does it present to the spirit—the fire that burns like fallen leaves: the fire liberated by dying—the threat of total annihilation (death or nothingness), but it keeps the spirit domesticated in its house, close to its fire, and more fearful than ever of the night sky.

This final domination of black is transformed into another element—cold—and is made the subject of the next poem, "The Snow Man." In it, the mind has been outside for a long time in the annihilating element in order to see the things of winter without thinking

> Of any misery in the sound of the wind,
> In the sound of a few leaves,
>
> Which is the sound of the land
> Full of the same wind
> That is blowing in the same bare place
>
> For the listener, who listens in the snow,
> And, nothing himself, beholds
> Nothing that is not there and the nothing that is.

That the two qualities, black and cold, were interchangeable was still in Stevens' mind in the 1940's, for they appear in "Burghers of Petty Death": "These are small townsmen of death,/ A man and a woman, like two leaves/That keep clinging to a tree,/Before winter freezes and grows black." And that anyone who has "been cold a long time" is in fact dead would seem to be the point of the ending of "Like Decorations in a Nigger Cemetery," the very title of which nicely associates black and death: "Can all men, together, avenge/One of the leaves that have fallen in autumn?/But the wise man avenges by building his city in snow." In the context of the whole poem, the snow city is a mithridatic cemetery. It is not, then, a physical death that is required but a spiritual one. And this spiritual death, since it is not misery, does not produce a towering heroism. Cold and nothingness continue dominant at the end, just as black continued dominant at the end of the preceding poem and at the end of "Three Travellers Watch a Sunrise."

But cold is dominant at the beginning of "The Snow Man," and—except for an alternation of sight, hearing, and then sight again—this poem records one simple form of consciousness, the most extreme instance of the "Nota" in "The Comedian": "his soil is man's intelligence." In "The Snow Man" the soil and the sap that comes out of it are so frozen that one cannot even imagine any fluid moving in the spruces and the junipers, "shagged with ice" and "rough in the distant glitter/Of the January sun." All that the soil can produce is a hollow sound in the wind, a sound of bareness.

The third, and last, of these important poems of death and nothingness, "Thirteen Ways of Looking at a Blackbird," also begins and ends in the snow; and the permanence of the blackbird in this otherwise destructive element makes it the chief instance of a persona who has indeed a mind of winter. This poem —perhaps the most systematic exercise in epistemology that Stevens ever indulged in, as William Keast's exegesis of it testifies[4]—deserves careful explication. The poem begins in a cold, sublime setting. The speaker, or looker, is moved or disturbed by the eye of the blackbird. The rhythms are arranged to make "eye" a prolonged utterance to correspond with a prolonged and fascinated attention to it. The speaker is made self-conscious by the little blackbird's eye; he is not so much looking at the blackbird as being looked at by it; and the consequence in Part II is that the speaker looks at himself. It is a troubled look; he finds that the blackbird has trebled his consciousness; and a blackbird sits, alien and intrusive, on each of the three branches. These birds are objects of knowledge to which the life sap of the tree contributes nothing; they are not leaves or blossoms or fruit.

In Part III, however, the autumn winds blow the blackbirds out of the tree and out of the speaker's mind; or, if the winds are not quite that powerful, there is a conflict between blackbird and winds, such that, as in "Domination of Black," the internal fear is externalized. There is a difference, however: the threatening blackbird is now threatened. It is as if the hemlocks were to sway and fall in the twilight wind. The autumn winds would also blow the leaves out of the speaker's mind-tree; death comes to everything that lives. If the blackbird is simply the sensible aspect of experience—what will not be submerged in a sublime response to mountains in Part I and what will not be regarded as a product of the mind in Part II—then the bird is like the hemlocks in "Domination of Black": it is the quality, black, so bound up with a thing, bird, that it is more than the metaphor (black is a bird). It is a new thing with a life and death of its own. Here, in Part III, the death of the blackbird seems to parallel that of the speaker, as in "The Misery of Don Joost": when the speaker and his senses die, so will the blackbird. Furthermore, the blackbird is no more real than the speaker; the speaker's mind and the blackbird are imitations of something more real. They are both phenomena which enact some kind of pantomime, a dumb show. In the words of "Metaphors of a Magnifico," this show "will not declare itself." But it is an imitation of something; it responds to something outside itself. The blackbird may be an alien squatter in the mind-tree and known only *in the mind*, but it, like the mind, is apparently at the mercy of death. Something, therefore, must sustain them and make them as they are, just as something like a cold wind brings their existence to an end.

Since the import of Part III seems to be that the speaker need worry only about his own death and not about the blackbird, Part IV begins with a proposition about life: "A man and a woman/Are one." This is a perfect instance of what is called "the sexual myth" in "Men Made Out of Words." But just as sexual union makes two lovers feel that they are eternally one, the blackbird, an equally primary fact of life, shows itself to be part of that unity. So another action begins: just as the avid, ominous look of the blackbird punctured the sublime unity of the speaker and the twenty snowy mountains, now the blackbird intrudes into the harmony of love. Again intrusion causes the speaker to reflect; Part V, like Part II, begins with "I," and the speaker finds that now he is of two minds rather than three. Does he prefer palpable form or impalpable meaning? The question arises because the blackbird must have contributed *something* in its unity with the man and the woman. Was it the merely sensible aspect of sex, or was it some meaning beyond the sensible aspect? Perhaps the blackbird is closer to the thing in itself after all.

Part VI disposes of the latter possibility by sending the blackbird out of the room. Or rather, the speaker is inside a winterbound room and the blackbird shows only its shadow. As in

"Domination of Black" the room is the mind, altogether bounded by its perceptions. Beyond them, in the winter of reality, there is only a transparent world of icicles—bare herbs saying barbar-barbar. This might be, perhaps, the Newtonian universe of measurable qualities: that is, all that the external world presents, intelligibly, to the glassed-in understanding. But the blackbird, even when lost to direct perception and made to fly between the sun, the "unthinking source," and the window of perception—the blackbird is still palpable; it still casts a shadow. Not only that, but the protected, glassed-in, paranoiac mood (much like that in "Domination of Black") traces in that shadow "an indecipher-able cause." All that one can depend on, internally, is a mood and a perception; and they point to a cause that will not declare itself. All that the external world presents is meaningless measur-able qualities—meaningless, that is, in any effort to find an ulti-mate meaning. So, a palpable quality—a mood and a shadow, a perception with its own characteristic charge of feeling—remains regnant.

Thus the speaker becomes of one mind; what the blackbird contributes to the unity of sex is its palpable quality. In the strength of this certitude the speaker thrusts out and becomes active; he scolds some ascetics who have visions of golden birds and tells them that what they are really looking for is the pal-pable quality of sex. Haddam, though it sounds Near Eastern, is a town in Connecticut, mentioned again in "The River of Rivers in Connecticut"; these are Puritan ascetics or their summer art-colonist descendants. The Near Eastern quality may be in-tended, nevertheless, for in "The Blue Buildings in the Summer Air" Stevens speaks of Cotton Mather's notion of heaven in this way: "Over wooden Boston, the sparkling Byzantine/Was every-thing that Cotton Mather was/And more."

Reflecting on the self-delusion that the speaker points out in Part VII, he now finds two seemingly conflicting attitudes which he is not to choose between but to synthesize. Unlike the thin men of Haddam, who know divine accents, he knows accents that are only noble—that is, they remain human. And *like* the thin men of Haddam, he knows "lucid, inescapable rhythms"; but, most unlike the men of Haddam, he knows that the blackbird is involved in all knowledge. From this conclusion he can further conclude in Part IX that the palpable marks the horizons of everyone's experience: when the blackbird is disappearing over the horizon of his circle of knowledge, it is entering someone else's. Now that he no longer has a sense of his mind's being divided within itself, he has a sense of its being separated from other minds; but in Part IX he also has a sense of its having something in common with other minds: the palpable—that is, the blackbird. He can see at the edge of his circle the same blackbird that others can see at the edges of theirs.

Part X, then, follows Part IX as something like an experiment in empathy. The bawds of euphony—who concentrate on only the pleasant aspects of sense experience and who do not even go to the bother of projecting those pleasant aspects into a golden heaven—are as far from the thin men of Haddam, and from the speaker, as it is possible to imagine. And yet the speaker speaks confidently of what they "would" do if they saw blackbirds "flying in a green light." After examining how his experience differs from and coincides with that of the thin men of Haddam, he is able to imagine how painful it would be for people who indulge their senses so thoroughly as the bawds of euphony do to encounter a raw, unmitigated fact like the blackbird. They would "cry out sharply." And this sharpness enters his customary reflection as a fear so thoroughly understood that he can refer to himself as "He," rather than as "I," as he has, at regular intervals hitherto (parts II, V, and VIII; now, at the same interval, XI).

After having expathized with such a different sort of consciousness as that of the bawds of euphony, he is able to look at himself as at another person. He sees himself afraid of breaking up his elegant, mobile, but fragile mind-room; and he sees himself projecting that fear into whatever is palpable about the mind itself: "The shadow of his equipage." The situation is the reverse of that in Part VI, where he was watching the shadow of the blackbird on the icicle-filled window. All his knowledge is thrown into doubt; possibly he knows nothing about the blackbird *by observation.* But one notices that he is able to tell the difference between the shadow of his equipage and blackbirds; he must be observing himself from some point of view from which this difference is discernible. And since, at least for the purposes of keeping this a pure case of projection, his point of view cannot be one from which he can observe the blackbird directly, he must be seeing himself from the point of view of the blackbird itself.

In Part XII, he is at one with that alien fact, the blackbird; and the moving, reflecting element is no longer his mind but a river. All he could be sure of in the experience of riding over Connecticut in a glass coach was that he was moving. If he distrusts his fear of breaking his fragile mind, he is left with a simple transparent flux: a river. From his point of view, knowing no more than that all things move in their characteristic elements, he knows that if the river is moving, the blackbird must be flying. It is either a logical inference or a pictorial necessity, as in a Japanese print. But after the ultimate shake that he himself has given to his confidence in his judgment in Part XI, the sureness with which he says "The blackbird must be flying" suggests that he has permanently identified himself with the blackbird.

And yet, in Part XIII, the speaker suggests that he will die but the blackbird will go on. It will continue to get darker and darker ("The Domination of Black"); it will continue to snow ("The Snow Man"); but the blackbird will sit in the evergreen cedar, an implacable everblack. This conclusion is not a logical or pictorial necessity, put in the theoretical present: "The river is moving./The blackbird must be flying." It is a historical fact put in the particular past: "The blackbird *sat*." The reader is back where he began. As I suggested at the beginning of this explication, this blackbird has been cold long enough to have a mind of winter. Indeed, the blackbird is the sort of persona that Stevens was later to call "the necessary angel of earth," which says:

> . . . in my sight you see the earth again,
> Cleared of its stiff and stubborn, man-locked set,
>
> Rise liquidly in liquid lingerings,
> Like watery words awash;

The water image has echoes in Crispin's experience at sea, as well as in the experience of the speaker in Parts XI and XII—the glass coach and the river instances—of "Thirteen Ways of Looking at a Blackbird." It also bears on the image in Part XIII, except that there the liquid is falling and turning solid and the tragic drone is becoming more tragic. The difference between this image in Part XIII and that of "the necessary angel of earth," which appears in the poem, "Angel Surrounded by Paysans" (first published in 1950), illustrates the difference in mood between Stevens' early and late poetry.

To sum up the import of these three central poems of death and nothingness, reality has a quality of blackness or coldness, or both. The effect is that of death or nothingness. It is nevertheless palpable. And it remains constant and dominant while all else falls, freezes, melts, rises, falls. It is also nameless, or rather, so closely bound up with some *thing*—hemlocks, blackbird—that it as a quality cannot be abstracted from that thing. This absolute concreteness gives death or nothingness an absolute wildness: try as it will, the mind cannot tame it; and, in the attempt to tame it, the mind shares the fate of all the other elements. It too is drawn into the gulf and passes through a cycle of forms, now hard and brittle, as if made of glass or ice; now broken up and melted down and flowing, like a river.

IV *Life*

The poems celebrating life and imagination in *Harmonium* all say, in effect, that "Death is the mother of beauty," which is the central implication of the figure of the wheel or cycle of forms. This cyclical movement is best illustrated in the water image in "Peter Quince at the Clavier." Water appears first in the second movement, which is slow and reflective. The rhythm, marked by past and present participles, pauses and lingers, while Susanna softly searches "The touch of springs," finds "Concealed imaginings," and sighs "For so much melody." Her body, not her mind, meditates; and so one is prepared at the beginning of the fourth movement for the surprising inversion of the usual notion of immortality: "Beauty is momentary in the mind—. . . But in the flesh it is immortal." But more important, her body meditates in "green water, clear and warm"; and this prepares the reader for the liquid images of immortality, culminating in the image of extreme unction at the very end.

At the beginning of the series of variations on this theme, the body's beauty is said to live after the body dies as "evenings die, in their green going,/A wave, interminably flowing." This evening goes on and on over the face of the earth as the earth turns. This sets the pattern, not only of the imagery—of eternal flux—

but of the rhythm and the tone, which are calm and meditative.
In rendering the first three variations—evenings, gardens, and
maidens—the voice of the poem intones with a deliberately
sacerdotal timbre. The liquid sensuality of the second movement,
insofar as it continues into the fourth, has lost its note of girlish
self-indulgence; it has become colder, purer. "So gardens die,
their meek breath scenting/The cowl of winter, done repenting."
In the context of flux, one may imagine that, when the snow
melts in the spring, the scent of the garden's meek breath will
again be released but, if possible, even more meekly. The purity
of snow leads quite normally to the purity of maidens, who also
have their season: dawn, which, like evening, is a quality of light
that flows on and on like a wave. Finally, "Susanna's music
touched the bawdy strings" of the elders, but they died for their
crude desires by the same legal decision that established Susan-
na's purity. Now her purity is a purifying "sacrament of praise"
for those who let her music play "On the clear viol of her mem-
ory." "Viol," in the context of death, purity, sacrament, and im-
mortality, is probably a pun on "vial"; the sacrament suggested is
extreme unction. The prayer blessing the oil begins, "Send forth,
we pray thee, O lord, thy Holy Spirit, the Paraclete, from
heaven, into this fatness of oil, which thou has deigned to pro-
duce from the green wood for refreshment of mind and body."

So the "green going" of the bathing pool and the evening
light continues to the end of the poem and beyond, if there is
a real sacrament involved. But what is most interesting is that
what began as an excess of emotion that leaves Susanna quaver-
ing ends as such a purified and immortal movement of her feel-
ings that, even in a metaphor of the circling of the mornings and
evenings and seasons, it triumphs over Death. It must be recalled
that Stevens placed this poem *before* "Thirteen Ways of Looking
at a Blackbird"; Death has, therefore, the last important word in
the first edition of *Harmonium*. But Susanna's softly passionate
purity does continue to play in the memory, so that the last lines
in "Thirteen Ways of Looking at a Blackbird" can be read with a
little less despair:

> It was evening all afternoon
> It was snowing
> And it was going to snow.
> The blackbird sat
> In the cedar-limbs.

With Susanna's beauty in mind as an ever-flowing sacrament of final purification, this part of the wheel of the elements—the falling of light and snow—seems less intimidating. There is a brighter part of the wheel, and a simpler, less anguished form of consciousness that goes with it, represented by the evergreen cedar limbs.

This consciousness is characteristically, in Stevens' early poetry, a woman's. Hence the woman in "Sunday Morning" simply will not accept "The holy hush of ancient sacrifice," when "comforts of the sun are enough." For her the implacable blackbird is replaced by "the green freedom of a cockatoo"; her encounter with death is so gentle that it is no surprise that there is no theme of purification in the poem. "Death is the mother of beauty," and not an evil or even a harsh mother:

> Although she strews the leaves
> Of sure obliteration on our paths,
> The path sick sorrow took, the many paths
> Where triumph rang its brassy phrase, or love
> Whispered a little out of tenderness,
> She makes the willow shiver in the sun
> For maidens who were wont to sit and gaze
> Upon the grass, relinquished to their feet.
> She causes boys to pile new plums and pears
> On disregarded plate. The maidens taste
> And stray impassioned in the littering leaves.

Susanna does not stray impassioned in the littering leaves when she encounters Death, in the form of the lecherous old elders, who threaten to accuse her of adultery, a capital offense, if she will not submit to them, and who carry out their threat. The woman in "Sunday Morning" is not especially concerned with pain and purity in death, but with the oppositions between God and man, permanence and change, boredom and joy. She stretches toward the opposite pole from that of the static nothingness represented by "The Snow Man," not as Susanna does, through an experience of a sudden and horrible fear of death— that is, through an experience that humiliates and purifies her —but through a just appreciation of the life of her senses, through a desire not to be bored, and through a confidence that she can find her happiness for herself without any special help from God. All that is required for Sunday Morning communion with the ultimate nature of things is the sun, "Not as a god, but as a god might be,/Naked among [us], like a savage source." Then Sunday Morning becomes simply "summer morn," and we do not evade the fact that

> We live in an old chaos of the sun,
> Or old dependency of day and night,
> Or island solitude, unsponsored, free,
> Of that wide water, inescapable.

The wide water referred to is that of which she thinks at the beginning of the poem as separating her from "silent Palestine,/ Dominion of the blood and sepulchre." It is like the ocean in "The Comedian," which "Severs not only lands but also selves"; it is not at all like the still water in which Susanna bathes. The wide water emphasizes isolation, and there is nothing sacramental about it.

And yet this woman, Susanna, and the several other young women in *Harmonium*, finally resemble one another more than they differ. They all rely on a fusion of their emotions and their perceptions to form out of themselves something to take the place of God. They are all versions of the Virgin, giving birth, in transcendent purity of instinct, to the "giant of the weather": the perceptual-emotional side of what in the dead of winter is nothingness but which at the height of summer is the principle of plenitude. The reader has met this giant, unnamed and not apparently gigantic in "From the Misery of Don Joost":

> "The senses and feeling, the very sound
> And sight, and all there was of the storm—
> Knows nothing more."

The "giant of the weather" is an expression of Stevens' late period, specifically from "Notes Toward a Supreme Fiction"; but there is such a giant in *Harmonium*, against whom three wanton Susannas concoct a plot: "The Plot Against the Giant." Odors, colors, and the "curious puffing" are supplied by the girls, thereby taming the giant; that is, they supply the perceptions, the perceptual and emotional side of the weather, the giant. Or, the giant, as God, is made wild, rather than tame by Ste. Ursule, who innocently offers him radishes as well as flowers: offers him her earthy aspect as well as her heavenly.

Similarly the "divine ingenue" in "Last Looks at the Lilacs" will finally be embraced by "the gold Don John," because "Her body [is] quivering in the Floreal/Toward the cool night and its fantastic star," patron of the gold Don John. This star is the evening star in "Homunculus et La Belle Etoile," which is "Good light for drunkards, poets, widows,/And ladies soon to be married." These "trembling ladies" also include the "women, swathed in indigo,/Holding their books toward the nearer stars,/To read, in secret, burning secrecies," whom the Polish aunt in "Colloquy with a Polish Aunt" cites as instances of the rule that "Imagination is the will of things."

Among these ladies one may also find "Florida, Venereal Soil," who is addressed thus: "Donna, donna, dark,/Stooping in indigo gown/And cloudy constellations,/Conceal yourself or disclose/Fewest things to the lover—/A hand that bears a thick-leaved fruit,/A pungent bloom against your shade." She is then, too, the "timeless mother" in "In the Carolinas" whom the poet asks: "How is it that your aspic nipples/For once vent honey?" And she replies, "The pinetree sweetens my body/The white iris beautifies me." She is "the goldener nude" of "The Paltry Nude Starts on a Spring Voyage"; she "Will go, like the centre of sea-green pomp,/In an intenser calm,/Scullion of fate,/Across the spick torrent, ceaselessly,/Upon her irretrievable way."

There are still other examples, but before I look at them, let me note that this woman occupies a central position in Stevens' poetic *mundo*—so central that in *Notes* she becomes his "green . . . fluent mundo" itself. A composite figure, she resembles Venus (Venereal soil; the center of sea-green pomp), Demeter (timeless mother), the Virgin (the divine ingenue), and, as will be soon evident, the Muse. She resembles all these divine beings in purity and in the power of her perceptions to create the world anew; but she also appears in perfectly human guises, as Susanna, for example, and as the woman in "Sunday Morning." Susanna, however, undergoes what is virtually an Assumption, since at the end of the poem her flesh becomes immortal and a sacrament. The woman in "Sunday Morning" has a more Protestant form of apotheosis: "Divinity must live within herself." But the effect is the same: she gives birth to the weather:

> Passions of rain, or moods in falling snow;
> Grievings in loneliness, or unsubdued
> Elations when the forest blooms; gusty

Emotions on wet roads on autumn nights;
All pleasures and all pains, remembering
The bough of summer and the winter branch.
These are the measures destined for her soul.

Since the weather, or the seasons, is the principal poetic
progeny that Stevens, as he shows himself in Crispin, wants to
create, the woman who can produce these for him is, inevitably,
his muse. This is already hinted in the sacramental function of
Susanna: her purity will inspire praise for her beauty, which is
also the beauty of the green evening, as well as for the perpetual
dawning represented by her maidenhood. Ste. Ursule, as a saint,
has the role of inspiring her form of piety, which is possibly
that of Freya, the Norse goddess of love and beauty, who ap-
peared in Sweden under the name Old Urschel and who wel-
comed the souls of dead maidens (hence the eleven thousand
virgins). The "women swathed in indigo" in "Colloquy with a
Polish Aunt" are explicitly replacements for "saints from Vora-
gine,/In their embroidered slippers."

But none of these women accomplishes quite the spectacular
epiphany and transfiguration of the ordinary that Vincentine
accomplishes in "The Apostrophe to Vincentine." Vincentine be-
gins "so small and lean/And nameless" that she is indistinguish-
able from the paltry nude whose spring voyage is "meagre play."
But Vincentine comes nearer: she shows herself to be "as warm
as flesh,/Brunette," and finally "Voluble," "walking" and "talk-
ing." The effect doubles and redoubles:

And what I knew you felt
Came then.
Monotonous earth I saw become
Illimitable spheres of you,
And that white animal, so lean,
Turned Vincentine,
Turned heavenly Vincentine,
And that white animal, so lean,
Turned heavenly, heavenly Vincentine.

The repetitions, and especially the repetitions of "turned,"
should remind the reader of "Domination of Black"; in "The
Apostrophe to Vincentine" the purpose and the effect are quite
contrary to the purpose and effect in "Domination" though not

a direct opposite; for Vincentine does not transfigure Death, but monotony: that is, what can be treated as the vulgar. In "Anatomy of Monotony" an older version of Vincentine—her mother, perhaps—is able to see the death, or nothingness, underlying this monotony:

> She walks an autumn ampler than the wind
> Cries up for us and colder than the frost
> Pricks in our spirits at the summer's end,
> And over the bare spaces of our skies
> She sees a barer sky that does not bend.

But, as in the case of Susanna, this awareness of death is probably not accidentally associated with an implied fecundity:

> The body walks forth naked in the sun
> And, out of tenderness or grief, the sun
> Gives comfort, so that other bodies come,
> Twinning our phantasy and our device,

The sun is no doubt the father, but (usually) the earth is the mother. The twinning is what is meant in "The Apostrophe to Vincentine" by "Then you came walking,/In a group of human others,/Voluble."

All these women serve as muses; but they fill that role best by contributing to an understanding of the one woman who is addressed as a muse in "To the One of Fictive Music." They do this by exhibiting ways in which this sort of woman is both divine and human, but more human than divine. Hence, as I have suggested, all these celebrations and praises of this sort of woman are best described as transmogrified hymns to the Virgin.

The woman of "Fictive Music," in spite of her extravagant titles as superhuman sister, mother, and love, wears on her head "No crown . . . simpler than the simple hair." The muse must be human because man's birth has separated him from "the wind and sea" and yet has left him in them "until earth becomes,/By being so much of the things we are,/Gross effigy and simulacrum." He tries to reunite with nature, but all his efforts only succeed in making nature seem like himself—and only a muse who is like man in this respect can help him out of his perverse predicament.

"Yet not too like." The muse must "endow/Our feignings with the strange unlike, whence springs/The difference that heavenly pity brings." For instance, when the good Lord heard Ste. Ursule's low accord and "felt a subtle quiver,/That was not heavenly love,/Or pity," the Lord's human lust makes his being God and his being an object of Ursule's abject devotion more strange—more strangely unlike man than his Godhead would have been had that been all he had. Heavenly pity, what would normally be expected from God in this situation, would bring the difference: it would be the strange unlike from which the difference springs.

Another instance of the difference that springs from heavenly pity is in "Anatomy of Monotony."

> The body walks forth naked in the sun
> And, out of tenderness or grief, the sun
> Gives comfort, so that other bodies come,
> Twinning our phantasy and our device.

Man may guess that these other bodies are more like himself than like his fantasy; but, being twins of our fantasy, they are also unlike. The reader is now in a better position to understand the important transition in "The Apostrophe to Vincentine": it was when she came walking "In a group/Of human others,/Voluble" that the speaker received what he knew she felt. *Then* "Monotonous earth I saw become/Illimitable spheres of you,/and that white animal, so lean,/. . . Turned heavenly, heavenly Vincentine." It is when the vision multiplies into *human* others—and the vision itself thereby becomes the chief instance of something strangely unlike humanity—that man can see his possible perfection. For this reason at the end of "To the One of Fictive Music" the poet cries out, "Unreal, give back to us what once you gave:/The imagination that we spurned and crave."

At the beginning of the poem, "the one of fictive music" is addressed as one of "the sisterhood of the living dead"; and in this idea of the muse as a mercifully detached personage there is an important image of the meeting of life and death. Both the idea and the image are of the essence of "Lunar Paraphrase," which begins, "The moon is the mother of pathos and pity," and goes on,

> When, at the wearier end of November,
> Her old light moves along the branches,
> Feebly, slowly, depending upon them;
> When the body of Jesus hangs in a pallor,

> Humanly near, and the figure of Mary,
> Touched on by hoar-frost, shrinks in a shelter
> Made by the leaves, that have rotted and fallen;
> When over the houses, a golden illusion
> Brings back an earlier season of quiet
> And quieting dreams in the sleepers in darkness—
>
> The moon is the mother of pathos and pity.

Death is imminent in this poem. It is the wearier end of November; the moon's light is old, and it moves along the branches "Feebly, slowly, depending upon them." The body of Jesus is "Humanly near" because it "hangs in a pallor"; and the moonlit pallor is as much a cause of pity as the hanging. The figure of Mary, which occupies a central position in the poem, is so cold that, instead of reaching out in mercy and love to all, she shrinks in a shelter of leaves that have rotted and fallen. Far from being the fecund mother, abundant and overflowing with good for all, she is forced to hide in dead things because her son, God, is dead. It is when God is dead and His mother shrinks from life that over the houses—shelters that are not made of fallen and rotten leaves—"a golden illusion/Brings back an earlier season of quiet/And quieting dreams in the sleepers in darkness." Compared with the golden illusion that is fostered by the darkness inside our solid shelters, the body of Jesus and the figure of Mary are too human; they are also strangely unlike what one wants to think of as human: a humanity that is at home in "an earlier season of quiet." "One must have a mind of winter/To regard" the hoar-frost on the figure of Mary, but one does not have a mind of winter when asleep in the dark in a warm bed. The moon gives Jesus no bed, and Mary a cold one. Such furnishings are like those which the poet asks the one of fictive music to wear: "On your pale head wear/A band entwining, set with fatal stones." Such furnishings man has spurned because they seem supernatural; but, for the same reason, he craves them. Unfortunately, man expresses his craving most of the time in a golden illusion—a nostalgic, sentimental escape.

I have said this is an important image—the image of the moon as detached and thereby merciful—since it sponsors the imagination in that way. It occurs, for instance, at important points in the two long poems "The Man with the Blue Guitar" and "Esthetique du Mal." In them, and especially in the latter, the image is elaborated; in the process the moon is almost abandoned, being too indulgent, too merciful. In "Esthetique du Mal" the moon gives way to the "grossly maternal," the earth-mother-muse who is less merciful because less detached. The moon, then, represents an extreme that the muse never reaches; and the strange unlike that she represents and produces are not so strange and unlike as Mary and Jesus.

The reader notices, for instance, that "the body of Jesus *hangs* in a pallor," in "Lunar Paraphrase; but in "Sunday Morning" the woman hears a voice that cried, " 'The tomb in Palestine/Is not the porch of spirits lingering./It is the grave of Jesus, where he lay." Hanging in a pallor, the body of Jesus is like a spirit lingering; having lain in his grave, Jesus is no longer alive, not even in the way of Susanna's immortality. The "wide water without sound" that separates the woman having her late coffee in a sunny chair from Jesus is not like "the green water, clear and warm" that carries Susanna's pure beauty on and on. Jesus is dead and buried, and Mary is now most notably the mother of the giant of the weather, or the mother of the human others that twin our fantasy: that is, she is a force for life; and, though she may herself be one of the living dead, she is by that very fact able to oppose death with beauty.

She could be the mother of Hoon. If there ever was a giant of the weather, Hoon is he. Hoon is the clear prototype of the central, romantic, idealistic character of the later hero; he says, "I was myself the compass of that sea:/I was the world in which I walked, and what I saw/Or heard or felt came not but from myself." But he also says that "there I found myself more truly and more strange." He makes this very clear at the start:

> Not less because in purple I descended
> The western day through what you called
> The loneliest air, not less was I myself.

That is, the purple and the palaz indicate that he is the king; "the loneliest air" indicates that he is all alone; and, therefore, if he *is* the world in which he walks, he would seem to be so all-inclusive that there would be nothing other than himself in comparison with which he could be strange or "myself."

The poem, then, presents a clear paradox: it is when he is the sun, the source and the identity of everything, that the poet is most unique and himself. It is, therefore, not a uniqueness that requires comparison with other beings coexisting, nor with antecedent and subsequent selves or with manifestations of the self. It is the uniqueness of self-sufficiency—indeed, the very lack of any need to receive definition by comparison and contrast. Hoon stands in the place of God, as when He spoke to Moses from the burning bush, saying "I am that I am." Nothing is stranger, *less nameable*, than this "I am."

This absolute self-identity is another central idea of Stevens' work, and it appears in his two most important long poems. In "The Man with the Blue Guitar" he says: "I am a native in this world . . . Here I inhale profounder strength/And as I am, I speak and move/And things are as I think they are/And say they are on the blue guitar." In "Notes" he says, "I have not but I am and as I am, I am." Each of these has somewhat different emphases, but the idea is essentially the same.

As Michael Benamou has pointed out,[5] Hoon is the transcendental half of the later hero figure, the quotidian half being the fool, Crispin, and "caliper" in "Last Looks at the Lilacs," and some others. As Hoon and Crispin are fused, Crispin's wife, the "prismy blonde," becomes the earth-mother-sister-mistress-muse that I have been confecting out of Susanna and the other virgins in *Harmonium*; but, when the "prismy blonde" achieves this status, she is only the mother of the hero. If she is anyone's mistress, then, she is the poet's and the sun's. This is a pagan holy family.

V *The Vulgar*

On first glance, the vulgar often seems to be Stevens' predominant theme. Crispin ends his career by celebrating the vulgar, trying to find in it the source for all the good and the glory of the seasons. And Crispin's Carolina rankness is a carefully chosen tone. One should note, for instance, the way in which the muse-figure that has been discussed is supplanted by a vulgar burlesque of it in "Floral Decorations for Bananas":

> You should have had plums tonight,
> In an eighteenth-century dish,
> And pettifogging buds,
> For the women of primrose and purl,
> Each one in her decent curl.
> Good God! What a precious light!

But bananas hacked and hunched.
The table was set by an ogre,
His eye on an outdoor gloom
And a stiff and noxious place.
Pile the bananas on planks.
The women will be all shanks
And bangles and slatted eyes.

The important thing here is the association, as in "The Come-
dian," of plums with decent curls—not the prismy blonde, but
her divine daughter-seasons with curls—as contrasted with the
association of bananas with shanks, bangles, and slatted eyes.
Equally important, the vulgar scene is set by an ogre whose eye
is "on an outdoor gloom." "Anatomy of Monotony" showed us a
similar grimness behind the monotony of autumn: "over the bare
spaces of our skies/She [earth] sees a barer sky that does not
bend."

What is involved here is two degrees of reality: materialism
and death. In "The Noble Rider and the Sound of Words," pub-
lished in 1942, Stevens speaks of "the pressure of reality" and
then gives what appear to be examples of this pressure: housing
projects and the radio: "We are close together in every way. We
lie in bed and listen to a broadcast from Cairo, and so on. There
is no distance. We are intimate with people we have never seen
and, unhappily, they are intimate with us. Democritus plucked
his eye out because he could not look at a woman without think-
ing of her as a woman. If he had read a few of our novels, he
would have torn himself to pieces" (NA, 18). He goes on to
talk about the labor movement as "a revolution for more pay."
And then he says that these are not examples of the pressure of
reality but examples of materialism, something that man gets
used to, like the weather, and that what he really means by the
pressure of reality is the pressure of war—of violent, unintel-
ligible death. World War II is completing "the collapse of our
system" which the Depression had begun; but, in order to do so,
war must be a pressure of reality much greater than that of
materialism. The difference in pressures is made vivid in "Anat-
omy of Monotony": beyond the weather that man gets used to
(like materialism) the mother earth sees "a barer sky that does
not bend" (like death or nothingness).

Stevens' idea of vulgarity did not change significantly during his career; perhaps his concept was the result of his own material success and his scorn for those who cannot satisfy themselves in matters of material comfort, or don't know what to do with money when they have it. His clearest statement of the latter alternative is, again, in "The Noble Rider and the Sound of Words." At the beginning of that essay he cites several examples of noble riders—the charioteer with a white horse of divine passion and a black horse of earthly passion in Plato's *Phaedrus,* Verrocchio's Bartolommeo Colleoni, Don Quixote—and then:

> There is in Washington, in Lafayette Square, which is the square on which the White House faces, a statue of Andrew Jackson, riding a horse with one of the most beautiful tails in the world. General Jackson is raising his hat in a gay gesture, saluting the ladies of his generation. One looks at this work of Clark Mills and thinks of the remark of Bertrand Russell that to acquire immunity to eloquence is of the utmost importance to the citizens of a democracy. . . . This work is a work of fancy. Dr. Richards cites Coleridge's theory of fancy as opposed to imagination. Fancy is an activity of the mind which puts things together of choice, *not* the will, as a principle of the mind's being, striving to realize itself in knowing itself. Fancy, then, is an exercise of selection from among objects already supplied by association, a selection made for purposes which are not then and therein being shaped but have been already fixed. (*NA,* 10-11)

In a poem of the 1930's Stevens calls this particular work of fancy "The American Sublime":

> How does one stand
> To behold the sublime,
> To confront the mockers,
> The mickey mockers
> And plated pairs?
>
> When General Jackson
> Posed for his statue
> He knew how one feels.
> Shall a man go barefoot
> Blinking and blank?
>
> How does one feel?
> One grows used to the weather,
> The landscape and that;
> And the sublime comes down
> To the spirit itself,

The spirit and space,
The empty spirit
In vacant space.
What wine does one drink?
What bread does one eat?

"The mickey mockers/And plated pairs" are "objects already supplied by association," selected "for purposes which . . . have already been fixed." Must one accept this with barefoot, country-yokel innocence? One can get used to it, as one gets used to the weather, and then one can get down to the real sublime, "the empty spirit/In vacant space." But what America has to offer for the empty spirit is worse than vacant space; and one is left with the question of a fitting sacrament: the simplicity of the need for wine and bread, in the face of what Tom Sawyer would have called a gaudy statue, leaves one at an absolute loss. The vulgar not only makes the blank space beyond it blanker: it taints and prevents the sacraments that might help one to confront death.

The vulgar taints by joining together fixed entities which can be counted on to elicit stock responses, not true ones: and thus it prevents a fresh perception of the flux of things—such as the green going of Susanna's evening—which acts as a sacrament that heals and purifies and enables man to confront death and nothingness without succumbing to them. For Stevens the essence of poetry is the fresh perception of life; his plainest statement about the function of poetry, again from "The Noble Rider and the Sound of Words," is that it "helps us to live our lives" (NA, 36). Crispin, for instance, shows the depth of his vulgarity by accepting death as simply the clipping of his relation with all possible wonder.

Poetry does not help "The Ordinary Women" to live their lives, not only because they do not seek out poetry for this or any other purpose but also because strictly speaking they have no lives. Using the terms that Stevens applies to the equestrian statue of General Jackson, their lives are neither of reality nor of imagination, but of fancy. Clark Griffith[6] has pointed out that these women are going to the movies. They go to get away from "dry catarrhs," "monotony," or what Stevens calls, in "The Man Whose Pharynx Was Bad" (a man with a catarrh), "the malady of the quotidian." Theirs is a mechanical substitution of guitars for catarrhs; and with the guitars are joined other fixed entities: palace walls, nocturnal halls, lacquered loges, and, most of all, the artificial moonlight of the movie screen. These women apparently have to stand up in the back and lean through windows; and this posture—in keeping with Stevens' regular use of windows to signify the separation of thought from perception—emphasizes the oversimplified and ready-made character of what they see.

These women see Hollywood's version of the heavenly marriage bed in which the characters are as simple as letters of the alphabet; they are strangely unlike only in that it is the Greek alphabet, but that unlikeness is as familiar as the word "alphabet" itself. They have no difficulty making the correct correlations, "beta b and gamma g"; and the "canting curlicues," say, of Valentino's sideburns, do not disguise the clear intention that these characters stand for boy and girl. (Beta Gamma used to be a common name for high-school-age church groups, meaning simply "Boys and Girls.") But then the musical accompaniment for the movie rumbles into its finale, calling it a day or returning the theater to overhead lighting ("The Moonlight/Rose on the beachy floors"); and then the ordinary women, looking into the theater from the standing-room-only part, see the actual coiffures of other, less ordinary women sitting in the theater. The sight of these jeweled hair-dos also elicits stock responses: "Insinuations of desire,/Puissant speech, alike in each." These insinuations and this speech make the guitars "dry." The women are drained of the juiciness of the heavenly marriage bed, and they are forced to return to catarrhs, which do not make them so painfully aware of their poverty and therefore act as a kind of anodyne to their desire.

With them there is no Schopenhauerian alternation of desire with the boredom of surfeit; there is no deep satisfaction or misery at either end of the cycle. The acceptance of the routine they know, signified by catarrhs, is as perfunctory and self-delusive as their vicarious consummation of heavenly marriage at the movies. These women are always poor, but they are never so deeply spiritually poor and miserable that they can imagine having a mind of winter ("The Ordinary Women" is placed between "The Snow Man" and "The Load of Sugar-Cane"). And they are never pure enough to partake of the sacrament of "The going of the glade boat" in "The Load of Sugar-Cane," which creates by metaphor a flowing, ever-new world of grass, rainbows, whistling birds, and "the red turban/of the boatman," which is far richer than any diamond-pointed coiffure.

Stevens uses the word "misery" in "The Snow Man" in the sense in which he ordinarily uses the word "poverty," especially in his later poetry. The most explicit statement of the relationship between the absolute poverty and the absolute wealth represented by "The Snow Man" and "The Load of Sugar-Cane" is in "The Sail of Ulysses":

> The self as sibyl, whose diamond,
> Whose chiefest embracing of all wealth
> Is poverty, whose jewel found
> At the exactest central of the earth
> Is need. For this, the sibyl's shape
> Is a blind thing fumbling for its form,
> A form that is lame, a hand, a back,
> A dream too poor, too destitute
> To be remembered, the old shape
> Worn and leaning to nothingness,
> A woman looking down the road,
> A child asleep in its own life.
> As these depend, so must they use.
> They measure the right to use. Need makes
> The right to use. Need names on its breath
> Categories of bleak necessity,
> Which, just to name is to create
> A help, a right to help, a right
> To know what helps and to attain,
> By right of knowing, another plane.

> (*OP*, 104)

"Just to name is to create a help": within "The Snow Man" itself one sees "the junipers shagged with ice,/The spruces rough in the distant glitter," and one does not think of any misery. The creation of such a help is an instance of the sublime, which as Stevens says in "Esthetique du Mal," is "Pain killing pain on the very point of pain." But it is also a purification that prepares one to accept his nothingness and that of the world, and so to accept such descriptions as "The going of the glade boat/Is like water flowing"—descriptions that go on from one resemblance to another in a circle, a rounding out of an emotional space in such a way that it no longer feels empty but is instead overflowing. It is nothingness transfigured, the renewal of the self working a new creation of the world.

Or, to return to the ordinary women, the difference between their poverty and that of "A woman looking down the road" in "The Sail of Ulysses" is that they never look down the road; they never yearn in vain. Instead, they indulge themselves in prefabricated escape fancies. They do not, childlike, go to sleep in their own lives: they never throw themselves absolutely on the resources of their own imaginations.

Following "The Load of Sugar-Cane," Stevens placed another poem devoted in part to the vulgar, "Le Monocle de Mon Oncle." The speaker addresses a woman who will not accept the fact that she is getting to be middle-aged and ugly. So the speaker mocks her with the names she wants to hear herself called: "Mother of heaven, regina of the clouds,/O sceptre of the sun, crown of the moon." These are indeed "mickey-mockers" and "plated pairs"; for, as the woman is now middle-aged, she may be a mother, but not of heaven; a regina, but not of the clouds. What had once been words of love—the second word in each pair opening up the kingdom of the beloved to the widest possible extent —are now words that come together like the blades of a guillotine, "the clashed edges of two words that kill."

Similarly, in the second stanza, the speaker is no longer a red bird, or, if he is, the choir he seeks to join no longer welcomes him. He knows this; yet the woman goes on pretending that he seeks her and she welcomes him in the same old way, still living in anecdotes of their blissful youth. In Stanza III he tries beards and coiffures as symbols with which to convey the fact that they have precious little with which to sustain the old feelings; but she comes to him with her hair undone, as if that were still attractive. At last in Stanza IV he tries the apple, and its short juicy life sums up the situation so neatly that in Stanza V he abandons the attempt to turn the old metaphors into magnifying mirrors in which the woman can see herself as she really is.

In the next four stanzas he looks for a metaphor of the fleetingness of youthful beauty and love which can somehow include the middle-aged condition of himself and his woman. That is, if the old metaphors don't apply, or apply only in a vulgarly fanciful way, then what does? In stanzas V, VI, and VII he hasn't much success. The furious star in the west—*la belle etoile*—burns only for fiery boys and sweet-smelling virgins; and the more earthy counterparts of that star—crickets—can be only a memory, not a present, living image of their desires and their "bond to all that dust." In Stanza VI the substance that prevails seems too much like a bald head, unless one dies young, like Hyacinthe, and becomes a perennially blooming flower. (Or like Susanna, a wave perpetually flowing.) In Stanza VII the conventional hope of purely spiritual beautitude shows itself to be too slow or uncertain in coming, like the help that in fact (not in television movies) might be on its way to the perishing lovers. And in the meantime, to change the figure, the Roman soldiers take their coarse burlesque of the Eucharist while Christ hangs on the cross. The honey of earth "both comes and goes at once." Stanza VIII finds that the only accurate image seems to be a version of the apple image that closed the first part of the poem (I-IV). They may be golden, in the autumn of their lives; but they are warty and rotting, and the permanent blue of the sky laughs at them. Stanza VIII then ends the effort to include the sweetness of youthful love in an image that accurately shows a middle-aged couple what they are.

In the last four stanzas the speaker tries frankly cynical metaphors. Beginning in Stanza IX, he suggests that what is needed is something noisy and deadly; in X, something merely sexual; and in XI, something with the quality of

> a pool of pink,
> Clippered with lilies scudding the bright chromes,
> Keen to the point of starlight, while a frog
> Boomed from his very belly odious chords.

These are the same old horns of the speaker's dilemma—the young and the fine versus the old and the coarse—turned into a cartoon. But the pool of pink and the odious chords are just as immiscible as "mother" and "heaven" are in the expression "mother of heaven" at the beginning of the poem. At the beginning of the poem the speaker asks if he isn't mocking himself alone, and the question is partly answered in Stanza XI: try as he will, he cannot evade an unhappy wedding of relatively fixed images. The conflict between youth and age, in the predicament of middle-aged would-be lovers, has a built-in vulgarity about it. The entire situation is, as it were, a reflection in the monocle of a French uncle, unmarried, cynical, and self-consciously a Fool.

Just as the sublime is "pain killing pain at the point of pain," the self-mocking monocle is an attempt to turn the vulgar against itself. The effect is similar to that of the sublime: the self is finally admitted to be nothing, as at the end of "The Snow Man," and as when the speaker refers to himself as "He" in Part XI of "Thirteen Ways of Looking at a Blackbird." Here in "Le Monocle," in the last stanza, the speaker admits that "Man proved a gobbet in my mincing world." His efforts throughout the poem have been to find an image of man heroic enough to include both young and middle-aged love. Now, admitting that no such image is possible, not even a brutally cynical one, he opens himself to a perception of fluttering things: and he finds that, even regarded as fluttering things, the blue pigeon of young love and the white pigeon of middle-aged love have more distinct shades than he had known them to have had. He is like Prufrock, who—once he has admitted that he is a Fool—can plainly make fun of himself and at last see the black and white, the life and death, of his situation.

Sharp as the speaker's perception of the distinct shades of his situation may be, he is stopped by that perception. He is no closer to a heroic image than Crispin was at the end of "The Comedian." The vulgar, then, is the great obstacle to heroism in *Harmonium*; and it continues to be an obstacle in *Ideas of Order*, Stevens' second book, which contains poems about the early Depression. By the same token, the vulgar is the great cause for comedy in *Harmonium*. Self-nullifying sublimity—as in "Domination of Black," "The Snow Man," and "Thirteen Ways of Looking at a Blackbird"—is not comic. There is a gaiety about "Blackbird"; but, when it is not somewhat grim, it is like the gaiety of the two Chinamen at the end of Yeats's "Lapis Lazuli." If all there were in *Harmonium* were the experiences of death and life represented by "The Snow Man" and Susanna, Hoon would be a hero—perhaps a tragic hero, but nonetheless a hero. Death would be his only adversary, but he would have Susanna for a mother-sister-mistress-muse. He could never be completely lost.

The vulgar interferes with a clear confrontation between life and death; and for this reason Stevens' hatred of it is intense. Crispin's last phase expresses some hope that the vulgar can be transfigured, and Stevens continued throughout his career to try to effect this metamorphosis. The attempt usually involved some wit, as in "The Ordinary Women" and "Le Monocle"; but I find a poised irony about both of those poems that does not appear in his two poems dealing with a vulgar Christian image of the afterlife, "Of Heaven Considered as a Tomb" and "A High-Toned Old Christian Woman." In these poems Stevens is clearly bitter, satirical rather than ironical, and—in the light of his primary reason for hating the vulgar—with good reason. It is precisely the vulgar Christian image of the afterlife that most taints and prevents any sacramental confrontation between life and death. If death is not death but a transport to a perpetual Sunday morning of the sort that the woman in "Sunday Morning" resents and rejects—that is, a comfortably sad and a comfortably ascetic idleness—then death cannot be stark enough to require any really intense life in opposition to it. Therefore, what Stevens does in those two poems about heaven is to join together one aspect of the fixed, vulgar image of heaven with an opposite notion, either of death or of life. In "Of heaven considered as a Tomb," it is of death.

The "interpreters" are probably like the exegete implied in "The Mechanical Optimist," who produces "the exegesis/Of familiar things in a cheerful voice,/Like the night before Christmas and all the carols." Such interpreters would be pleased to place those whose lives had a happy ending ("our old comedy") in the sky and to give each a lantern, and so account for the stars. But such interpreters would be aghast at taking the rest of the qualities of the night sky along with the two comforting ones. To say that it is a tomb, gusty, cold, even icy and that the motion of the stars suggests a perpetual, pointless search is to have gone to the movies with the ordinary women and there to have discovered the domination of black. It is, quite simply, to turn a spurious death into a real death. Similarly, "A High-Toned Old Christian Woman" turns a spurious into a real afterlife.

"Of Heaven Considered as a Tomb" begins in a polite, leisurely way and only at the end makes saucy suggestions. "A High-Toned Old Christian Woman" has from beginning to end the brisk tone of a butcher arguing with a customer about something that concerns them both—say, how to cut up meat:

> Poetry is the supreme fiction, madame.
> Take the moral law and make a nave of it
> And from the nave build haunted heaven. Thus,
> The conscience is converted into palms,
> Like windy citherns hankering for hymns.
> We agree in principle. That's clear. But take
> The opposing law and make a peristyle. . . .

In a Protestant scheme of things a heaven projected from the opposite of the moral law would be a paradise of sexual anarchy; and the speaker in the poem goes on to show not only that there is no absolute way of choosing between the two kinds of heaven—since they are equally plausible—but also that her heaven, the one in which her dead husband is supposed to be mortifying his flesh in order to remain faithful to her, may not be very different from its opposite. The "disaffected flagellants" may be having a kind of cosmic sauna. Thus poetry, the supreme fiction, makes its Nietzschean turn or wink, as in the Ste. Ursule poem, and makes high-toned old Christian widows wince. Nietzsche said of Heine, "He possessed that divine wickedness, without which I cannot conceive of perfection; I value men and races according to the necessity they have to imagine a god partaking of the nature of the satyr."[7]

The effect is the same as in "Of Heaven Considered as a Tomb": a false life is made to show its falsity by being shown to contain within it its opposite. Or, rather, what is false about this afterlife is the feelings that it is a projection of. They are not those of a healthy, generous, virile Christian conscience; they are those of a genteel, "high-toned," effeminate conscience, "Like windy citherns hankering for hymns." Such a conscience (and any devout Christian must wince at this use of "conscience") contains or projects such an ambiguous image of heaven because it is itself a dishonest and phony conscience. If it pretends to speak so simply of a dead man's chastity, it knows not whereof it speaks, not because dead men are not chaste but because in any case it is not that simple.

Thus Stevens satirizes vulgar images of the afterlife. Vulgarity and death would seem to be as immiscible in his mind as young and middle-aged love. And yet there is a poem in *Harmonium* which takes the vulgar and turns it into an image of spiritual poverty, of death, and even of a countervailing force of life. This poem, "The Emperor of Ice-Cream," may be the virile vulgarity that Stevens is indirectly referring to in the last parts of "The Comedian." Crispin himself does not fit this scene, which seems to be that of a wake in a brothel; but Crispin's tone is there. The tone of "The Emperor" is that of the quotidian that saps philosophers but also offers a humped return. Everything in the scene is rapidly breaking up or wearing away, but the very oldness of things becomes new, the poverty becomes riches, the vulgarity becomes life and death. In the first stanza these transformations are not so noticeable. There is something worn and sad about the muscular one, the dawdling wenches, and the boys bringing flowers in last month's newspapers. But even there the tone of absolute permission, the acceptance that comes as a command, and that the command of a metaphysical emperor of all Being and Seeming, transforms all these tawdry appearances into an image of the momentarily frozen stream of reality —that is, the image of ice-cream; they all become parts of a simple and delicious dessert which all people, vulgar or not, enjoy. The gaiety here is not satirical but childlike, which indicates the relevance of Stevens' comment that his daughter particularly liked ice-cream. The people in this scene are like children at a party, and in that sense they are like everyone else. Everyone cherishes those moments when somehow the flux is able to take an apprehensible form, moments of sheer delight in that momentary firmness, as well as in the liquefaction that immediately follows. In the very tasting, life melts upon the tongue; but the point of appetite comes only to the as yet unmelted moment. As children, the vulgar and the noble are one.

Thus prepared for this sort of transfigured ordinariness, the reader finds in the second stanza deeper delights: the dresser without all its knobs is itself partly undressed; the wench, while she dawdled, embroidered her shroud; and now her feet, horny from much dawdling, are cold but uncomplaining, indeed unspeaking, as if by protruding they ought to speak as the head did, now that all things are reversed. She too is at an unmelted moment, as unappetizing as Susanna was appetizing; but disgust can be as exquisite as appetite.

Again, Being itself, or Reality itself, is the most exactly fixed appearance which is yet one that will surely soon change. The first stanza concerns sex; the second, death; and both are instances of moments that perception automatically *fixes*, vividly. But the fix is so vivid precisely because these are moments of greatest change: conception and death. In the light of this lamp one can see that the occasion is not a wake; it is simply a party, perhaps in a brothel, at which a woman dies, or perhaps is murdered. The order to cover her face must come at the moment of death, not at some time long after, when there has been time to invite people to the party. The lamp is the lamp of appetite or disgust; it is therefore an expression of the most rudimentary will of things, the will of the emperor.

This will does not always express itself so clearly and delightfully. The two poems that precede "The Emperor," "Banal Sojourn" and "Depression before Spring," have for a theme the frustration of the will of the emperor. In "Banal Sojourn" familiar images of death and life are separated and vitiated by the malady of the midsummer quotidian. Here are the black trees of "Domination of Black" and the grackle of "Thirteen Ways of Looking at a Blackbird"; here is "That bliss of stars, that princox of evening heaven," La Belle Etoile; and here is "radiance running down, slim through the bareness," Vincentine. But the last two, the images of life, do not appear; sought in vain is "the sky unfuzzed, soaring to the princox." What prevents the appearance of life is satisfaction beyond the point of appetite: "Moisture and heat have swollen the garden into a slum of bloom./Pardie! Summer is like a fat beast, sleepy in mildew." Similarly, in "Depression before Spring." "The hair of my blonde/Is dazzling,/ As the spittle of cows/Threading the wind." Here the difficulty is not surfeit but appetite too long unsatisfied. These two poems that precede "The Emperor of Ice-Cream" describe the summer and winter extremes of the blunting or breaking of the point of appetite. The image of ice-cream is an image of midwinter spring or of midsummer fall: the cold that melts on the tongue.

There is yet one more variation on this theme; a variation that calls attention to itself by its singular representative, "Frogs Eat Butterflies. Snakes Eat Frogs. Hogs Eat Snakes. Men Eat Hogs." It is an image of a perpetual sapping by the quotidian, with no return. As the river suckles its banks, so "the hours of [the planter's] indolent arid days . . . seemed to suckle themselves on his arid being." If his soil is man's intelligence, this man's intelligence is a swinish passivity that permits his being to be suckled away by this dirty, greedy river which in turn is sucked away by the even greedier sea. This bleak view of Crispin's quotidian death is not only unproductive, it is positively destructive. It is not merely clipped, it is swallowed.

The vulgar contains its dangers as well as its potential riches. It was the most problematical element in Stevens' poetic experience. For, difficult as the poverty of nothingness and death may be, they are sharply, painfully, and finally richly *definite*; they cannot be blinked. In his later poems Stevens pushed this definiteness to its explicitly nameless extreme: the essences of both life and death are always so new and nameless, so unique, that they can be denoted only by a pointing gesture. The difficulty of the vulgar is precisely its indefiniteness—its overgrown or overfed, its drugged or sleepy quality: the vulgar is an automatic assembling of fixed, dead pieces of common experience. It may be a minor obstruction to the confrontation of life with death, but it makes all the difference in the world.

Stevens was painfully aware of his own entanglement with the vulgar. In a sense, the most central poem in *Harmonium* is "The Weeping Burgher."

> It is with a strange malice
> That I distort the world.
>
> Ah! that ill humors
> Should mask as white girls.
> And ah! that Scaramouche
> Should have a black barouche.
>
> The sorry verities!
> Yet in excess, continual,
> There is cure of sorrow.
>
> Permit that if as ghost I come
> Among the people burning in me still,
> I come as belle design
> Of foppish line.
>
> And I, then, tortured for old speech,
> A white of wildly woven rings;
> I, weeping in a calcined heart,
> My hands such sharp, imagined things.

That the hair of his blonde is dazzling as the spittle of cows in "Depression before Spring" is a good example of one strangely malicious distortion: that ill humors should mask as white girls. Only by such an excessive statement can one pierce the plated pairs (*good* humors go with white girls) and confront one's own death and so find one's own life. Perhaps no queen comes in slipper green; perhaps one does not find one's life; but at least one has made the necessary preparation.

This necessary preparation, however, is hard to live with. The weeping burgher in accepting his own death not only becomes a ghost in comparison with the people who are losses still burning in his heart, but he also intensifies that burning, by making loss itself elegant, until his heart is reduced to powder, so that his tears bring no relief, and his hands have become so sharply imagined, in order for them to cut their foppish line through the vulgar facade, that, when he seeks to console his weeping eyes with them, he only makes his pain sharper. The second stanza of "The Emperor of Ice-Cream," for instance, makes a vulgar death an elegant instance of the will of things; to transfigure one's own death, say, at the loss of someone's love or of someone one loves, in the same way, is to make one's own death exquisitely painful. When the vulgar is allowed to let itself go to such an extreme that it becomes its opposite, the burgherly self does likewise. The self-mocking, self-nullifying monocle of "Mon Oncle" breaks in his own piercing hands. The Fool reveals his inherently tragic character.

CHAPTER 2

The Middle Period

B ETWEEN 1924 and 1930 Stevens published nothing; and when he did publish again, he spoke with a different tone. Although he seemed to have entered upon a middle period, there is a sense in which Stevens had no middle period. For, from the time he began to publish again in 1930 until the publication of "The Man with the Blue Guitar" in 1937, he appeared to be groping for a way out of the spiritual depression caused by the economic Depression. The means of Grace that worked in *Harmonium* no longer sufficed, and he had found no new ones. Nor did "The Man with the Blue Guitar" really end this period of groping; it was only his first extended vision of the way out. Until the publication of *Notes Toward a Supreme Fiction* in 1942, most of his poems lack the lightness of touch, the characteristic gaiety of *Harmonium*; but they have not yet acquired the thick, sure tone of his later poetry, which in a very real sense begins with "Notes Toward a Supreme Fiction" and never surpasses that poem in the generosity of its temper and its achievement.

The tone of his poetry in the 1930's was most of all one of self-conscious meagerness and timidity, a hopeless yearning for transcendence or escape. What had to be escaped or transcended was the vulgar. But now it had become a "wintry slime" of "men in crowds": it had become

> these sudden mobs of men,
> These sudden clouds of faces and arms,
> An immense suppression, freed,
> These voices crying without knowing for what,
> Except to be happy, without knowing how.

The vulgar had become an all-embracing and all-depressing element, and also a real economic and spiritual problem.

The vulgar in *Harmonium* was a poetic problem, perhaps

Stevens' chief poetic problem, but it was not the primary pressure of reality. It was an element that rather annoyingly intervened between the imagination and reality, and Stevens was justifiably proudest of the poems in which he was able to transform it from an obstruction into a magnifying mirror or a lens or even a jewel. Only after the war had begun in Spain in 1936 was Stevens able to transform the vulgarity of the Depression into something translucent.

Stevens tried in vain to accomplish this transformation before the war by bringing his experience to an inner, personal (rather than an outer, social) focus. The Depression, as an oppressively all-embracing vulgarity, had the opposite effect: it scattered and diffused his feelings. It importuned him to sympathize with a plight and a people for whom he normally had only feelings of disgust. It was, in fact, such a heavy distraction that the only way Stevens could even begin to bring his experience to an inner focus was to try, again in vain, "To expunge all people and be a pupil/Of the gorgeous wheel." He wished he could ignore the Depression, and he yearned for the transcendent self-sufficiency of Hoon, who contains the gorgeous wheel of sun and sea. But this reaction came before "The Man with the Blue Guitar," which stands as Stevens' great declaration of independence for his spirit: his insistence, at a crucial point in his development as a poet, on the inner personal focus as the only proper perspective for poetry. And this inner focus cannot transform the vulgar into its opposite unless it focuses the experience of war.

In order to see how urgent this need for an inner focus was, the reader must first look at the poems immediately preceding "The Man with the Blue Guitar": those in *Ideas of Order* (1935) and the long poem "Owl's Clover" (1936). Usually disregarded by critics because they are not very good, these poems reveal Stevens in a crucial transition. In direct proportion to their badness, they show Stevens' poetic problems more clearly, and so I shall give them more attention than is customary.

I   Ideas of Order

Stevens apparently put the poems in *Ideas of Order* in a significant serial order. At the beginning[1] he deliberately says "Farewell to Florida"—farewell to the lush Southern scene in

which Crispin settled down—and as a matter of poetic duty re-
turns to the North to confront the unavoidable reality of the De-
pression, "a slime of men in crowds." This reality is unavoidable
because there is no other; and, in the series of poems from "Fare-
well to Florida" to "The Idea of Order at Key West," he finds
it so difficult to make light of "a slime of men in crowds" that
he approaches but never seriously assumes the pose of a revo-
lutionist.

This is a surprising role for Stevens to approach; and, to un-
derstand why he does, one must realize how much the slime of
men disgusted and entrapped him. In the first poem in *Ideas of
Order*, "Farewell to Florida," he grimly faces the fact that "the
violent mind/That is their mind, these men, . . . will bind/Me
round." In "Ghosts as Cocoons," the second poem, the bride will
not appear to redeem "This mangled, smutted semi-world hacked
out/Of dirt," in spite of the fact that "Those to be born have
need/Of the bride," because they are prevented from being born
by "The fly on the rose" and the "ghost of fragrance falling on
dung." By "those to be born" Stevens probably means people
like himself, but the things that prevent regeneration (which
must never cease, in Stevens' poetic religion) sound very much
like the slime of men in "Farewell to Florida."

The only appropriate thing to do about this slime is to "ex-
punge" it—as the poet suggests in "Sailing after Lunch." In that
poem the slime of men and their semi-world hacked out of dirt
are what make the "historical sail" heavy and thus prevent the
boat from rushing brightly through the summer air. This dirt,
then, is the romantic that has remained; in other words, it is the
fixed elements of fancy: the vulgar. It does not change, in the
way that "the light wind worries the sail" and that "the water is
swift today." It is like the "Too many waltzes" that have ended
in "Sad Strains of a Gay Waltz": it is "so much motionless
sound." But in "Sad Strains" the crowds of men become more
than an impediment. They speak out, inchoately but actively;
and they supplant "mountain-minded Hoon," who had previously
been able to expunge all people. The men in crowds are more
than a fixed, dirty weight; they even resemble, in their vulgar
way, the mountainous figure of the hero that Hoon becomes.
That is, they are described as "These sudden clouds of faces and
arms."

In "How to Live. What to do," the eighth poem in *Ideas of Order*, there is an image of a heroic height, a rocky mountain top: "The ridges thrown/Like giant arms among the clouds." "Chocorua to Its Neighbor" and "A Primitive like an Orb," two later poems, have similar images. But the difference between the heroic and the vulgar image is clear enough in "Sad Strains" and in "How to Live. What to Do": it is the difference between clouds of arms and arms *among* clouds—the difference between mist and rock.

Whether slime or mist, these men cry out helplessly for happiness, and their cries join with the increasing blare of disbelief. The situation seems so hopeless that Stevens turns to satire of a curiously revolutionist sort. "Dance of the Macabre Mice" offers a *danse macabre* as a successor to the gay waltz, and the interesting thing about it is that it is as fixed and vulgar as the old waltz was: "At the base of the statue, we go round and round." But fixed and vulgar as the mice's dance is, the statue is more so; it is like the equestrian statue of Andrew Jackson, Stevens' arch example of the American vulgar sublime. Although the mobs of men are reduced to mice, they are less absurd than the product of the public fancy that they are subverting. Stevens is definitely on the side of revolution here, primarily a revolution in the imagination, of course; but it also has a political dimension: "Whoever founded/A state that was free, in the dead of winter, from mice?" But he is careful to reassert, in "Meditations Celestial & Terrestrial," the poem that follows, his deeper allegiance: "We hardened ourselves to live by bluest reason/In a world of wind and frost" and so to accept, in a bitter, cynical way, revolution; "But what are radiant reason and radiant will/To warblings early in the hilarious trees/Of summer, the drunken mother?"

He returns to satire again, however, in the next poem, "Lions in Sweden." After saying he cannot use the traditional images of the civic virtues—faith, justice, patience, and fortitude (weeping burgher that he is)—he asks whose fault it is. Somehow these images, or images like them, are all that the soul is made of; and the soul, therefore, "hankers after lions, or, to shift,/Still hankers after sovereign images." The title suggests that this hankering may be true of even the most rational men; for Sweden, more than any nation, tries "to live by reason." And yet Sweden has a king; and ever since Sweden's great warrior king, Charles XII, was called the Lion of the North, lions have been prominent in the country's political iconography. At the end of the poem Stevens makes the cynical suggestion that perhaps the lion is the trouble since the only lions commonly seen and believed in any more are caged ones. Hence they should be sent back to their common supply center, Hamburg, which is celebrated for precisely this demythologizing function in Apollinaire's bestiary, which was illustrated by Dufy.

But again the poet can't leave the matter on a note of despair; in the next poem, "How to Live. What to Do" he finds a heroic height where

> There was the cold wind and the sound
> It made, away from the muck of the land
> That they had left, heroic sound
> Joyous and jubilant and sure. . . .

The "muck of the land" is "a slime of men." The poem insists that one can at least momentarily glimpse a state of mind like that in the life and death poems in *Harmonium*.

It is only momentarily, however. In the next poem, "Some Friends from Pascagoula" Stevens is again making fun of sovereign images, this time the American eagle. It is an image dazzling only to "a kinky clan," by which he apparently means a credulous people. And yet he calls them friends, just as he sympathizes with the credulity of Swenson in "Lions in Sweden" and with the mice in "Dance of the Macabre Mice." His sympathy in all cases is cynical or satirical. The conflicts are ones in which he cannot wholeheartedly engage; they are all between vulgar people and vulgar images. Although the health of the whole world may be at stake, it is not a problem with which a meditative poet can deal.

What the meditative poet can deal with is what it is "To be one's singular self," the subject of the next poem, "Waving Adieu, Adieu, Adieu." To be one's singular self is "to stand still" and receive what spirit one has from the sun. Then one is always crying farewell to one's past self, to all fixed and therefore vulgar images. And, since one is at best always saying farewell while standing still, one needn't have left Florida in order to say "Farewell to Florida." Hence "The Idea of Order at Key West"—the title poem of *Ideas of Order*—is a significant return to

Florida. The sea in that poem embodies as much bleakness as the heroic height in the North. More important, that poem actually renders the inner personal focus which the preceding poem, "Waving Adieu, Adieu, Adieu," only talks about. "Whose spirit is this? we said, because we knew/It was the spirit that we sought. . . ." It is not the spirit of the singer nor of the sea, for the sea has no spirit. But "when she sang, the sea,/Whatever self it had, became the self/That was her song, for she was the maker."

> Then we,
> As we beheld her striding there alone,
> Knew that there never was a world for her
> Except the one she sang and, singing, made.

The inner focus is not in the self of the poet but in the world of his poem: what Stevens later called "my green, my fluent mundo." This is an intensely personal world, and yet—as the reader knows from "To the One of Fictive Music"—it also has something of the strange unlike. Stevens writes in "The Idea of Order at Key West":

> The sea was not a mask. No more was she.
> The song and water were not medleyed sound
> Even if what she sang was what she heard,
> Since what she sang was uttered word by word.
> It may be that in all her phrases stirred
> The grinding water and the gasping wind;
> But it was she and not the sea we heard.

This is the only poem in *Ideas of Order* that succeeds in restoring something of the order of *Harmonium*. It does it, I believe, partly by using the image of the sea, which Stevens discovered later[2] in "Farewell to Florida," to be another good image for the men in crowds:

> The men are moving as the water moves,
> This darkened water cloven by sullen swells
> Against your sides, then shoving and slithering,
> The darkness shattered, turbulent with foam.

This metaphor is not explicitly used in "The Idea of Order at Key West"; but, placed as it is after "Farewell to Florida" and after all the references to the slime of men that has to be expunged to enable one to sail brightly and to the muck that one must look away from in order to see the heroic height, the image in the poem of the sea as having a grinding, repetitive voice seems to belong to the same family of images. Further, there is associated with the sea in "The Idea of Order at Key West" an image of workaday practicality which suggests that Stevens was actually trying to incorporate the common man's pursuit of happiness into the singer's creation of order. At the end of the poem the poet asks his companion why, after the singing ended, the light of the fishing boats "Mastered the night" and gave order to the sea. The answer seems to be that the "Blessed rage for order" expresses itself first in the self-sufficient, solitary *mundo* of a Hoon or of the singer in this poem, and then, and only then, in the practical, workaday lives of men in crowds. The sea is, therefore, both an economic and a spiritual problem and resource; and it is made such a comprehensive metaphor in order to alleviate the burden of the Depression.

But the metaphor cannot do the job assigned to it. It is only in a far-fetched sense that fishermen can be imagined as "sudden mobs of men" or even "men in crowds." Fishermen are still, to many people at least, romantic; and the lights on their boats are hardly comparable, say, to Section 7(a) of the National Industrial Recovery Act. If anything, the lights on their boats remind one of the end of "Sailing after Lunch:"

> To expunge all people and be a pupil
> Of the gorgeous wheel and so to give
> That slight transcendence to the dirty sail,
> By light, the way one feels, sharp white,
> And then rush brightly through the summer air.

That is, the lights on the fishing boats are an image of light and of sailing more than it is of people and the depressing problems that they present. Stevens still could not have it both ways: if he re-established the order of *Harmonium*, it was by turning away from the problem of the Depression. He could not look within his own poetic *mundo* and there transmute the world of men in crowds—not yet.

In the next series of poems, from "The Idea of Order at Key West" to "Academic Discourse at Havana," Stevens looks into the one possible way by which he might find a bond with men in crowds: through organized religion. Organized religion is the common man's poetic *mundo*; and, if it happened to coincide with the poet's, then he could find the common man within his own *mundo* and could deal with the common man and his problems poetically.

I have already commented on the first of this series, "The American Sublime." After recognizing in it that "the mickey mockers/And plated pairs"—the fixed elements in such things as the statue of General Jackson—are worse than nothing as any sort of sacrament, as any sort of means of transforming the threat of death into the promise of life everlasting, the question still remains, "What wine does one drink?/What bread does one eat?" The next poem, "Mozart, 1935," provides an answer, but it is no help:

> Poet, be seated at the piano.
> Play the present, its hoo-hoo-hoo,
> Its shoo-shoo-shoo, its ric-a-nic,
> Its envious cachination.

This seems to be a command to succumb to the mickey mockers, the ric-a-nickle-plated pairs. This appearance grows as the poet is further commanded to play a *divertimento*—not as background for polite conversation but for the sound of stones on the roof— or a concerto, with the same sound as that of the orchestra. But there is a tension, from the start, even in the posture of the poet seated at the piano, like ·that of Peter Quince at the clavier: these sounds—the ric-a-nic, the stones on the roof—cannot fit with the *divertimento* of the polite past, nor even with the concerto of the future. (As the reader will see in "Owl's Clover," Stevens believed that Basilewski's "Concerto for Airplane and Pianoforte" was a bubble that "bulged before it floated, turned/ Caramel and would not, could not float.")

As the poem proceeds, the tension almost breaks into satire: "Be thou the voice,/Not you. Be thou, be thou/The voice of angry fear,/The voice of this besieging pain./Be thou that wintry sound/As of the great wind howling,/By which sorrow is released,/Dismissed, absolved/In a starry placating." Shelley's "Ode to the West Wind" is no doubt the master pattern for this sublime identification with the destructive element, but Shelley was not Mozart; and it is Mozart that the poet is really being called to emulate:

> We may return to Mozart.
> He was young, and we, we are old.
> The snow is falling
> And the streets are full of cries.
> Be seated thou.

Although Mozart was considered too modern in his time, he was a classicist, a perfector of existing forms. And although he was at the height of his powers during the French Revolution—a time which, like the Depression, was to Stevens "the end of one era of the imagination and the beginning of another" (*NA* 21)—he expressed no compulsion to "be thou/The voice of angry fear." Mozart represents experience perfectly rendered into an abstract, classical form; and to be like him in 1935 with the ric-a-nic and the stones upon the roof is impossible.

"Mozart, 1935" somehow remains poised, tragically, on the edge of satire and cynicism without toppling over. It says to the question at the end of "The American Sublime" ("What wine does one drink?/What bread does one eat?"): "Poet, be seated at the piano." That is, nothing as formalized and perfectly realized as a sacrament or as Mozart's classicism can be made to incorporate and transfigure the experience of the Depression. But one must try. One must "Be seated."

There is a remote possibility that "Snow and Stars," the next poem, is intended as a piece of *buffo* such as young Mozart might have appreciated, but it is far too slapdash to really qualify. The conflict, repeated in each tercet, is between a sentimental first line and two cynical lines that follow it—much like the rather lame satires already discussed ("Dance of the Macabre Mice," "Lions in Sweden," and "Some Friends from Pascagoula"). That game of satire is up, at least for Stevens, whether in the manner of ironical sympathy for social revolution or a Mozartian farce. The bottom of despair in this matter is expressed in "The Sun This March," the next poem and the one with which Stevens broke his six-year silence. It was printed soon after the crash in 1929. It ends with the only plea that Stevens ever made for help from a personage who represents, in an abstract, ideal way, organized religion: "Oh, Rabbi, rabbi, fend my soul for me/And true savant of this dark nature be."[3] The rabbi is asked to fend the poet's soul. The light he brings must have the sovereign majesty of "lions coming down." It is, in other words, an ultimate knowledge.

But this knowledge is to no avail. "Marx has ruined Nature,/ For the moment," in the next poem, "Botanist on Alp (No. 1)"; and it is in Nature that Stevens is closest to God. Therefore, it requires a painter like Claude to bring Stevens close to the God of organized religion, for this artist painted "A world that was resting on pillars,/That was seen through arches." That perspective brings a poet like Stevens near "To the central composition,/ The essential theme." But, ever since Marx, Nature has been merely a material cause, nothing to apostrophize, and nothing that provides a *noble*, let alone a divine, end toward which to build. "Yet the panorama of despair/Cannot be the specialty/Of this ecstatic air." It can't give to Stevens "The poem of long celestial death," in the next poem, "Botanist on Alp (No. 2)"; but it can't give despair either, because there is still the possibility of an earthier poem, "As of those crosses, glittering,/And merely of their glittering,/A mirror of mere delight."

That possibility remains secondary, however, for the two questions with which "Evening without Angels" begins ("Why seraphim like lutanists arranged/Above the trees? And why the poet as/Eternal *chef d'orchestre?*") imply that someone has asked the poet and his poetry to address themselves to common beliefs, to "the poem of long celestial death." The earthier poem of delight in the mere glittering is not spiritually nourishing to common people but is rather a kind of élite religion, or substitute for it. "Evening without Angels" is largely devoted to making more explicit, and more dull, the gist of "Botanist on Alp (No. 2)." In doing so, however, it penetrates to some more elemental physical facts underlying conventional Christian symbols. For instance, as a "botanist" in the preceding poem, the poet might take an interest in the glittering crosses as "trees"; but that is not so plausible a source of that symbol's interest and power as "the rounded moon" is for haloes. The rounded moon is a physical and psychological fact that literally illuminates the entire imaginative process. It creates "arches and their spangled air," "rhapsodies of fire and fire,

> Where the voice that is in us makes a true response,
> Where the voice that is great within us rises up,
> As we stand gazing at the rounded moon.

The moon, in other words, provides the "central composition, the central theme" that Claude rendered: it creates a world resting on pillars, seen through arches. The master architect, however, is the sun, Stevens' true Creator, which is celebrated in the next poem, "The Brave Man," and which, if it represents an organized religious experience, represents that of the American Indian, as Babette Deutsch has observed.[4] That the sun can provide pillars is made explicit in the next poem, "A Fading of the Sun": spiritual help is available to those who "cry and cry for help" "Within as pillars of the sun,/Supports of night."

Thus the sun provides not only the pillars of a church, or a porch to heaven, but also the sacramental food; or rather, it makes the ordinary food of life good and sweet. The sun is, therefore, not only a source of mere delight, as when it makes the crosses glitter, but also a source of real spiritual (and physical) strength: it is a power as well as a good. It lacks nothing, for those who will accept it, as a complete successor to the Christian God. For instance, in the next poem, "Gray Stones and Gray Pigeons," only the sun can make the archbishop live up to his name: "bishop" comes from the Greek, *episcopos* (watcher), and one may suspect Stevens, in the context of the architecture of the cathedral, of punning on "arch," so that the archbishop is an arch through which God watches man, or through whom man in turn sees God. Only in his colored robes, though, does the archbishop enable the sun god to use him this way. Then the pigeons fly, suggesting the third member of the Trinity, as the sun and the archbishop suggest the first two members. The sun not only supplants the Christian God in this poem but actually makes out of its visual effects a casual trinity.

"Winter Bells," however, indicates Stevens' belief that the common man worships the sun in an altogether vulgar way when on vacation in "one of the little arrondissements/Of the sea" in Florida. The sun worship that he has been suggesting in "Botanist on Alp (No. 2)," "Evening without Angels," "The Brave

Man," "A Fading of the Sun," and "Gray Stones and Gray Pigeons" is an élite religion that—as he says in his essay "Imagination as Value"—cannot take the place of Biblical religion for most people:

> It cannot be said that the Bible, the most widely distributed book in the world is the poorest. Nor can it be said that it owes its distribution to the poetry it contains. If poetry should address itself to the same needs and aspirations, the same hopes and fears, to which the Bible addresses itself, it might rival it in distribution. Poetry does not address itself to beliefs. Nor could it ever invent an ancient world full of figures that had been known and become endeared to its readers for centuries. (*NA*, 144)

A little farther on Stevens says that the poetic imagination "tries to penetrate to basic images, basic emotions, and so to compose a fundamental poetry even older than the ancient world." For the poet, this attempt often implied a primitive poetry like "The Brave Man"; but, more characteristically, it implied an esthetic transformation and rejuvenation of conventional Christian forms. The primitivism involved in this esthetic revivification is explored at length in "Like Decorations in a Nigger Cemetery." For the moment, the reader must be content with the conclusion of "Academic Discourse at Havana": that ultimately the moon alone, without our intervention, may interact with "the old casino"—Claude's architectonic world of faith—and give man the definition and the incantation that he desires.

Such definition and incantation are a possibility, however, and not an actuality: ". . . the great poems of heaven and hell have been written and the great poem of the earth remains to be written" (*NA*, 142). All that has occurred is the decadence of the old religious myth and, finally, in this century, an inability to give any serious credence to the romantic myth (it "Passed like a circus"), and now man lives with an insistence that he live without imagination:

> Politic man ordained
> Imagination as the fateful sin.
> Grandmother and her basketful of pears
> Must be the crux of our compendia.
> That's world enough, and more, if one includes
> Her daughters to the peached and ivory wench
> For whom the towers are built.

Here Stevens is probably punning on "pear" to include the sense of "the plated pairs" in "The American Sublime"—a punning that is made explicit in "Forces, The Will & The Weather." In the latter poem "The pair yellow, the peer" stands for the perfect identity of measurable properties on which mechanical empiricism depends and against which Stevens opposes the imperfect and therefore fecundating resemblance on which poetry depends, both in that poem and in his essay, "Three Academic Pieces." Perfect identity is like "Grandmother and her basketful of pears" in that it is a fussy, infertile matching of sense impressions (all the pears she might bring to one of her daughters would be equally ripe). This monotonous kind of scientific realism is supposed to be "world enough, and more" if one includes the muse of the ivory tower; that is, if society excludes the poet from any direct relation with its life. That the muse of the ivory tower is a daughter of our mechanical-empirical, utilitarian grandmother is confirmed by a remark in Stevens' preface to William Carlos Williams' *Collected Poems, 1921-1931*:

> What, then, is a romantic poet now-a-days? He happens to be one who still dwells in an ivory tower, but who insists that life would be intolerable except for the fact that one has, from the top, such an exceptional view of the public dump and the advertising signs of Snider's Catsup, Ivory Soap and Chevrolet Cars; he is the hermit who dwells alone with the sun and moon, but insists on taking a rotten newspaper. (*OP*, 256)

The ivory tower is part of a society so "political," in a utilitarian "scientific" way, that it regards the poet as a superior kind of refuse; he is on a level with other forms of conspicuous waste, such as advertising. Therefore, "The burgher's breast . . . Must be the place for prodigy"; but, even there, all that actually seems to be left for the poet to work with is "mere sound." Stevens accepts this material, however; and he concludes the poem with the possibility of the moon and the old casino interacting without the help of the poet and providing man with the definition and incantation that he desires. Nevertheless, "Academic Discourse in Havana" leaves one with a bleak foreground, and the poems between this one and the end of *Ideas Of Order* are black poems. This color of despair emerges into the title of the climactic poem, "Like Decorations in a Nigger Cemetery."

"Nudity at the Capital" and "Nudity in the Colonies": These two couplets play with the oddity of nudity, or rather, of quiddity. The colonial Negro complains to his master in the capital of the white mother country that he is, as his scientifically sophisticated master has taught him, essentially an elaboration of an innermost atom, and therefore cannot be completely naked (unless completely decomposed, as in a cemetery). If man is at bottom an atom, any offense given by his backside should be comparatively superficial. Then the "woolen massa" expostulates with the "black man" that, if he wants to express his innermost self most, he should, in the tropical colonies—where the master's woolens are as unfitting as the Negro's nudity was in the Northern capital—go naked, rather than assume the false character imposed by the latest fashions.

This combination in the white master of staid propriety for himself at home and romantic honesty for his black charges in the colonies, set off against the superficially westernized Negro's combination of scientific honesty at the capital and falsely imitative white propriety at home, neatly epitomizes the impasse for the imagination which is confronted with a decadent civilization still caught between an escapist romanticism and a barbarous science. The impasse is born lightly, but it is no less an impasse. Even if the couplets are read as games that the poet is playing with "mere sound," playing "bottom" against "atom" and "pseudonymous" against "anonymous," the poet must follow the law that he found in "Academic Discourse in Havana": "It [the poet's function of mere sound] causes him to make/His infinite repetition and alloys/Of pick of ebon, pick of halcyon." The unruffled wit with which he plucks out these couplets does not conceal the ebon in his pick.

"Re-statement of Romance": If blackness is what the poet feels he is up against, this poem makes no effort to make it, as Stevens says a poem must, "a particular of life thought of for so long that one's thought has become an inseparable part of it or a particular of life so intensely felt that the feeling has entered into it" (*NA*, 65). The night is left as merely a background against which each solitary self throws out only a pale light and against which the interchange of two personalities is a pale and comfortless exchange, compared with the traditional romantic situation of the night's being in sympathy with lovers.

"The Reader": Even the book offered to the solitary poet by the blank night "bore no print/Except the trace of burning stars/ In the frosty heaven." Even the stars, which are not black and which traditionally give men some direction or hope, give the poet nothing but the sense that they, like everything else, fall back to coldness.

"Mud Master": This poem recalls "Ghosts as Cocoons"; everything is ready for spring, but no spring appears. Here the mind is likened to a muddy river and to a pickaninny, a small miserable rejected child of the mud; and the poet tells the mind with unconvincing assurance that the far off shaft of light is both "the mud master" and "the peach-bud maker." Coming as it does after "The Reader" with its burning, falling stars, this image of a shaft of light is not reassuring. Admittedly "the master of the mind" must work both ways, must be both dark and light; but here there is no balance, just as there was no balance, no rage for order to balance the chaos, in "Re-statement of Romance" and in "The Reader."

"Anglais Mort à Florence": As "Mud Master" recalls "Ghosts as Cocoons," this poem recalls "The Sun This March," only still more hopelessly. For in this poem the poet's becoming dark is not a change over a period of a year but a change over a period of a lifetime. The poem sums up the mood of the three poems which precede it: "But he remembered the time when he stood alone." In other words, "Before the colors deepened and grew small," he could have felt or thought his way into harmony with the night, either in a relationship of love with another person or in one with a book. He could have made the mud his element as much as he could make "new banks/Of bulging green" his element. It might have been a frightening element, as in "Domination of Black" or "Thirteen Ways of Looking at a Blackbird"; or in "Like Decorations in a Nigger Cemetery"; it might be a sharply frustrating one, as in "Depression before Spring," or a numbing, boring one, as in "Frogs Eat Butterflies. Snakes Eat Frogs. Hogs Eat Snakes. Men Eat Hogs," or in "The Man Whose Pharynx Was Bad." But in each of these *Harmonium* poems, the element is thought or felt through until the poet is one with it. In "Anglais Mort à Florence," as in the three poems preceding it, there is simply an uneven opposition without interaction between the blackness and the only slightly less "dark nature" of the poet.

"The Pleasures of Merely Circulating": Again, in a rhythm as tinkling and almost-cynical as that of the two couplets that began this series, the poet tries to thumb his nose at his plight. "Do the drummers in black hoods/Rumble anything out of their drums?" No, unless the interchangeability of Northern, Central, and Southern European children or climates, at one season or another, is "classical" in the sense that it describes a perfectly endless circle of repetitions. But this use of the word "classical" is pseudonymous; what is being expressed here is an anonymity that is meaningless, not classical. A dead spirit in a deadly round of weathers is a nameless spirit, whereas, although a doomed spirit like that of Achilles fell as the leaves fall, his lively resistance to death was marked at least by a mound and at most by a poem.

"Like Decorations in a Nigger Cemetery": In each of the first two series of poems in *Ideas of Order* the poet's spirit reaches a certain depth of despair or satire before finding a way of penetrating the gloom with some imaginative order and light. Thus "Some Friends from Pascagoula" precedes "Waving Adieu, Adieu, Adieu" and "The Sun This March" precedes "Botanist on Alp (No. 1)." "The Pleasures of Merely Circulating" might be read as "Waving Adieu, Adieu, Adieu" without its clue to the direction in which order can be sought. Correspondingly, "Like Decorations in a Nigger Cemetery," the poem which carries the poet to some kind of redemption, must find its own way; and, proportional to the deadness of the dead end in which the poet finds himself, it is a comparatively long and severe way. It might be called a way out of Hades.

The fifty stanzas of the poem can be grasped more easily as ten groups of five stanzas each. The over-all plan of the poem can be summarized roughly as follows: Present poetry is unruly because it deals with unexpected change (stanzas 1-5), as opposed to religion (6-10), nature scientifically understood (11-15), and old art (16-20), which make fixed predictions of change. The realism of modern poetry is neither sentimental nor cynical (21-25) because the summer that satisfies our yearning begets the winter of our desire (26-30). Poetry as the unity of summer and winter is thus "a finikin thing of air" (31-35), as new as the next biological development in man (36-40). But poetry must not try to conceal the mechanism of evolution as common, conventional projections do: by defying the mechanism (41-45). On the contrary, it must make itself out of the elements that threaten to destroy those mechanical projections (46-50).

The way out of Hades appears then to be through a rather blind confidence in biological evolution. Biological evolution operates in a dialectical way, evolving fixed forms which, by resisting the forces of change within them, destroy themselves and give way to the next development. This concept explains the title: if the Negro is regarded as a lower form of life than man is—hence the word "nigger"—the fitting gaiety with which he decorates his death prefigures the higher form of life, the full manhood, which will descend from him: the afterlife of our imagination is the imagination of the future. The poet, in the darkness of his spirit, feels like a "nigger" dead and buried, prefiguring his manhood on his tombstone.

It is, of course, of the essence that the example of the destructive element out of which the poet chooses to build his ideal city is snow—a deceptively white element. Snow can be as bright as the sun and can seemingly resist the melting heat of the sun. The poet even has the example of the Eskimo—another dark-skinned and, in the eyes of many, "inferior" form of man—who literally builds his house in snow. But an igloo is not a city, and it is also important that the poet identifies himself not only with the destructive elements (considers himself a barbarian) but with the highest degree of urban civilization. How this latter qualification is to be fulfilled remains to be seen; but at least for the moment the poet has found an image—snow—that is as realistic as the night, the mud, and the meaningless circulation in "Re-statement of Romance," "The Reader," "Mud Master," "Anglais Mort à Florence," and "The Pleasures of Merely Circulating"; and yet the snow image is not so depressing. It permits the poet to imagine himself allied with forces opposing the creative force of the sun without losing the sense of light, and with it the sense of lightness that seems to be more essential to his artistic well-being than any other sense. The snow also recalls his most successful metamorphosis of his imaginative self into the most deadly winter reality: "The Snow Man."

"A Postcard from the Volcano": If the wise man avenges one of the leaves that have fallen in autumn by building his city in snow and if the height of his civilization is manifest in the changes he works in the language, nevertheless children in the next era of the imagination will use the changed language bequeathed them with no sense of how it felt in the past to use it —just as one gets no sense of the experience of a volcano from the picture postcard one gets from someone who has actually had the experience. Thus the city built in snow will look dirty; its relation to the sun, which the poet found to be a source of hope, will seem superficial. The sun's gold will seem to have been smeared on like honey on dirty white bread. The dirtiness is there by the poet's deliberate effort to evade nothing. In "Like Decorations in a Nigger Cemetery," the "drenching weather" in Stanza 49 brings "the mud master" almost into contact with the "city in snow" in Stanza 50. Or, in "A Postcard from the Volcano," our quickness and the air's sharpness will seem just as cut off from the literate despair of the windy sky as the sunny snow at the peak of a volcano seems separated from the pile of refuse on which it lies, as long as the volcano is inactive. In fact, the sky's cry of literate despair suggests "a spirit storming in blank walls," and together they suggest that, to the children of the next era, the volcano was active in our time. What will remain in whatever changes in the language we may work will not be the bright hope of the snow and its alliance with the sun, but the black and furious hell we lived in.

"Autumn Refrain": The alliance of sun and snow, or of our quickness and the air's sharpness, seems as out of key with our present desolate situation as "The yellow moon of words about the nightingale." What is in key is "The skreak and skritter of evening gone/And grackles gone." So the ugly sound of the black grackles will remain; the yellow moon of words about the nightingale will be scraped out by "that desolate sound."

"A Fish-Scale Sunrise": In this mood, even the sun "rises green and blue," like a fish-scale; and "The clouds foretell a swampy rain." Despite all our dreams of "last night's dancing"—the music of the last era of the imagination—"The cocks are crowing and crowing loud": the world robbed of the old consolations has only harsh sounds and a small wet sun.

"Gallant Chateau": This poem seems to be a grim consolation

for the situation in "A Postcard from the Volcano." That the house one leaves behind—which is one to which one finally comes in his quest for the imagination of the future—should be an empty house is infinitely better than that one should find it already inhabited by a tragic heroine—say, a Clytemnestra—or a curse perfected in verse. Looking back at the two poems preceding this one, the reader can see that the "desolate sound" in "Autumn Refrain," and the "swampy rain" in "A Fish-Scale Sunrise" are not bad, but blank. Indeed at the very beginning of the sequence of poems between "Academic Discourse" and the end of *Ideas of Order*, the blackness in the poet's spirit is the result of an imaginative impasse. The poet regards this situation as good: according to Stevens' artistic creed, the poet's imagination is in a position to become most fertile when it seems to have no place to go, when what it confronts is empty.

"Delightful Evening": In fact, ironically, ordinary people, delighted by the wormy metaphors left over from the last era of the imagination, are quite right to call this a "delightful evening." The poet can use a more precise expression—"felicitous eve"—in addressing Herr Doktor, because he too is wise enough to be more concerned with the "reefs of clouds" on which the imagination is about to founder. And the poet can take consolation that the imagination of an era just passing is already rotting on the ground. Man is on "a very felicitous eve" of something new.

In summary, the inner focus in *Ideas of Order* that seemed to provide a tried and true way out of the tendency toward satire in the first series of poems ("Farewell to Florida" to "The Idea of Order at Key West") quickly led to another impasse: that of trying to get the feelings of the Depression into a classical form. Thus, in the second series of poems (between "The Idea of Order at Key West" and "Academic Discourse at Havana") the poet turns in despair to the forms of organized religion as the closest thing to an artistic composition of the ordinary man's inner life. But he finds that the only use he can make of the symbols of organized religion is as sensuous forms which finally, along with everything else, become part of an artistic composition satisfying only to an élite, even though it artistically penetrates to the basic images of the universal mind. Left with no vital relation to society as a whole, in the last series of poems (from "Academic Discourse at Havana" to the end of *Ideas of Order*) he tries to find some source of confidence in the fact that we are on the eve of a new era of the imagination and that, as a man of imagination, he may be among the first to see what form man and his poetry may take. That is, the poet must be both as civilized and as primitive as possible to both submit to the natural changes occurring and make those changes work corresponding changes in the language.

It is worth noting in passing that, if Charles Henri Ford's society-column piece, "Verlaine in Hartford,"[5] has no other use, it documents Stevens' persistent interest in collecting primitive and little-known painters rather than the established ones. He may have wanted to discover himself to be such a civilized primitive. Certainly he was attached to the role of court jester (and to derivatives of that role), and the court jester might be called the archetype of the primitive civilized man—the man who has such a mastery of the restraints and rituals of civilized life that he can, when it suits him, break all the rules with impunity.

II   *"Owl's Clover"*

One rule that Stevens found that he could not break without jeopardizing his art is the one of remaining civilized enough to concentrate his experience within a definite form, so that the form becomes a *mundo*-self parallel with his own. In the one long attempt to break that rule and to get away with it, "Owl's Clover," he tried to see things altogether from the common man's point of view; and the consequence is an eternal identity between imagination and night.

"Owl's Clover" has five parts, each with a title. In the first part, "The Old Woman and the Statue," there are two projections: the white horses of the sculptor and the black failure to think in the old woman. The woman's inability to respond to the perennial transcendence supposed to be provided by art gives the poem its black beginning. This blackness reappears in different form in the middle part, "The Greenest Continent," and in the last part, "Sombre Figuration." It is the blackness of night suggested by the title of the poem, "Owl's Clover."

In the second part, "Mr. Burnshaw and the Statue," there are two reflections: that of the poet, who sees the statue and all such conventional projections as a dump heap; and that of the muses, who at first represent Mr. Burnshaw's revolutionary optimism by expressing an explicitly Shelleyan hope for the future, but who are a little later converted by Stevens' pantheistic realism into a pagan acceptance of the present. Thus, as usual, Stevens' reflection is virtually a rejection: to see conventional projections as a dump heap is to reject them.

In the third part, "The Greenest Continent," there is a confrontation of lingering religious and political projections with the rawest sense experience and with Death, deified as a serpent god, Ananke. The confrontation is acted out by the angels of Europe who are trying to conquer the natives of Africa and, finally, the god of Africa, Ananke. Thus the confrontation has both the social-satirical strategy of making the victory of nineteenth-century Christian colonialism a Pyrrhic one, and the artistic strategy of making the old projections reject themselves by committing mythological suicide.

The fourth part, "A Duck for Dinner," presents a false, two-world solution to the problem of what will take the place of the old projections: the new barbarism of communism. Communism is false because it offers an imminent millennial afterlife for the era of the imagination that is dying, a perpetual Sunday in the park, which is no more able to inspire confidence than the statue in the park. The statue, as an image of the sculptor and his age, has only a sentimental appeal to the men sprawling on the grass.

The fifth and last part, "Sombre Figuration," is a true acceptance of the world as it is; but it is a grim image of the world that is accepted. The subman in everyone projects a primitive like an orb, a sprawling portent in the sky that offers no hope for the future. It gives instead a black night of the imagination in which man should be realistically afraid. Such a black imagination is rich clover for the owl, the swift silent predator of the night. Stevens may even have had in mind the image in a less solemn poem on the same theme, "Dance of the Macabre Mice": the statue of the Founder of the State is covered with mice, not with men. Owls feed on timid creatures lying still with fear in the grass—like the men sprawling on the grass in the park.

III *"The Man with the Blue Guitar"*

In resistance to this self-imposed darkness, "The Man with the Blue Guitar" deliberately seeks a way by which the poet can honorably repudiate the unbearable burden urged on him by such exponents of socially conscious art as Mr. Burnshaw. This poem (henceforth to be called "Blue Guitar") has thirty-three stanzas and can be divided into three sections of ten stanzas each, leaving three extra stanzas at the end of the poem, each of which summarizes one of the three parts: 31, the first; 32, the second; and 33, the third. In the first ten stanzas the people command the poet to lift them out of their misery without changing them; and the poet replies that they want a mechanical, sentimental, materialistic composure and not nobility in the face of death, which is what his detached reflective art is concerned with. His art would only satirize them, or make them show how pathetic they are. Or, as it is summarized in Stanza 31, the old dream of a permanent and fixed paradise is no longer possible: man is too self-conscious ("the cock/Will claw sleep"), too wide awake to things as they are. In the second part, the poet, seeing only the people with their petty desires reflected in his imagination, wonders if he has any identity apart from that reflection, especially if, as pure reflectiveness (the pure power of reflection reflecting on itself), he reflects a world that is bare and beastly. But his bitterness at this possibility indicates some self-consciousness, some imagination, though perhaps it is an imagination no less pathetic than the escapist fantasies of the people. Or, as it is summarized in Stanza 32, if man will just get rid of the conception of self as immortal soul, he will feel the fruitful complementary relation between self and space and will be himself fecund with metamorphoses.

In part three, the poet shows how his imagination and its poetry embody the destructive as well as the creative forces of reality itself; therefore, his poetry is not an escape from but an affirmation of things as they are. Or, as it is summarized in Stanza 33, with the destruction of the old dream, with the sense of the inherent destructiveness of the imagination, and with the realization that waking, working hopes are inevitable, man will live on the bread of hope while he works each day, forgetting that the bread of hope turns into the stone of hopelessness on which he sleeps each night, dreamlessly. But there will be times when he chooses neither to work nor to sleep, but to play. Then he can freely oppose the pain (destructiveness) and joy (creativeness) of nature with their counterparts in his imagination, the imagined pine, the imagined jay.

If the reader looks at the poem as a whole in relation to the poems I have used as summaries of *Harmonium*, he gets a dramatic feeling of how Stevens' poetic problem had changed during the first six years of the Depression. Taking a point of view somewhere in the dirtiest, lowest, or poorest part of his external world ("his soil is man's intelligence" or the point of view of the blackbird), Stevens was able to reduce the spiritual world of decadent, idealistic pretentions and fears to a size and a shape that permitted him to see it as only a superficial, ephemeral repression. It enabled him to see the worlds of matter and spirit as parts of one world and then to see that with ironical detachment and levity. A world without the pressure of living people, it was peopled instead with personae—with representative romantic and realistic attitudes interacting with each other.

The most significant of these attitudes is that of the weeping burgher: the poet's sense of his own strangeness and self-exile. The blueness of the blue guitar would seem to be a similar expression of that sense of strangeness. But one notices the great difference between the "strange malice" of the weeping burgher and the blueness of the blue guitar. The burgher produces an entirely internal grief; it is a purely self-destructive posture. Like Prufrock and the courtly lover in "Le Monocle," the weeping burgher finally fixes and formulates his own absurdity more sharply and exactly than he does that of anything in the world around him.

The blueness of the guitar, on the other hand, far from being a realistic and self-effacing image of the artist's self, is an ostentatiously idealistic and romantic one. Decadent, romantic idealism had turned into its falsely bárbarous opposite, Marxist materialism; and what Stevens poked fun at in *Harmonium*—sentimentality, the vulgar—was now being taken seriously and for practical materialistic ends. Not by the same people, of course, and critics like Stanley Burnshaw did not regard themselves as sentimental, or even as romantic. But Stevens, in "Owl's Clover" and in "Blue Guitar," took great pains to revive and emancipate his own variety of romanticism by distinguishing it from the "grubby faith" of Communism. His strategy in "Blue Guitar" is thus the opposite of his strategy in *Harmonium*: in "Blue Guitar" he wants his strangeness to stand out above the mechanized sentimentality of his Marxist critics and the underpaid masses of which those critics were the self-appointed spokesmen. In "Blue Guitar" Stevens decided and declared once and for all his solution to the desperate dilemma revealed in "Mozart, 1935": he must be free to "practice Arpeggios," if nothing else; and, as we shall see, much of *Parts of a World* is devoted to just such practice.

It would be useful, also, at this point to see what happens to the "Blue Guitar" solution at the end of the sequence which it starts—that is, in "Notes Toward a Supreme Fiction." At the end of "Notes" there is the emphasis on routine or practice that gets an implicit treatment in stanzas 23-26 in "Blue Guitar." But a more important theme, and one that bears more closely on the artist's relation to society, is that of work, sleep, and leisure. In "Blue Guitar" Stevens carefully distinguishes the sun-driven working life of desire and sleep from the moon-driven "moments when we choose to play/The imagined pine, the imagined jay." In "Notes" the working life and the wants of workers get no attention at all; instead, there is a kind of family life, located in houses or in parks, and composed of the relations between mother and son, husband and wife, brother and sister. The central person being addressed is "ephebe," who is essentially a young poet—"The Figure of the Youth as Virile Poet"—but who is quite Spartan in his self-discipline and who has a close complementary relationship to the actual soldier of World War II. There is a planter whose labor is mentioned, but it is work like that of the young poet, inspired and essentially artistic. Even the sleep in the poem is the anxious, almost conscious sleep of the artist.

The only theme in "Notes" that approaches the desire-and-sleep theme in "Blue Guitar" is a subsection in each of the three main sections that treats of bygone romantic beliefs in a kind of touristic naturalness and ease of poetic activity—compositions that create themselves out of feelings of sweet weariness while walking around a lake or out of sexual passion. These, however, are clearly middle-class self-indulgences, and they show only a distant resemblance to the point-blank desire and sleep of the people in "Blue Guitar." Clearly, in "Notes" Stevens is no longer worried about his leisure-time discipline of poetry—as opposed to the grim work-sleep rhythm of the workers' lives.

After the reader has watched the development of the idea of

the hero in *Parts of a World*, he will be able to see in its entirety
the metamorphosis of the weeping burgher into the hero and
from that vantage point he will be able to see more clearly the
meaning in "Notes" of Stevens' concentration on a rigorous, ar-
tistic leisure—almost to the exclusion of the common life of
desire and sleep. Stevens in "Blue Guitar" declares his inde-
pendence from the writers and critics of the 1930's who insisted
that art be socially conscious—be written from a proletarian
point of view. He now felt free to "practice arpeggios" or, more
important, to pursue his sensibility, wherever it might lead. He
no doubt felt reassured by Picasso's statements in 1935, for he
uses a phrase from it in "Blue Guitar." Picasso's statement begins
and ends with light-hearted references to society's rejection of
the artist but is otherwise devoted to his own creative process.
The lines in "Blue Guitar" in which the quote appears are in
Stanza 15:

> Is this picture of Picasso's, this "hoard
> Of destructions," a picture of ourselves,
>
> Now, an image of our society?
> Do I sit, deformed, a naked egg,
>
> Catching at Good-bye, harvest moon,
> Without seeing the harvest or the moon?

The phrase which Stevens is translating here is *"une somme de
destructions"* and the whole passage is as follows: "Auparavant
les tableaux s'acheminaient vers leur fin par progression. Chaque
jour apportait quelque chose de nouveau. Un tableau était une
somme d'additions. Chez moi, un tableau est une somme de
destructions. Je fais un tableau, ensuite je le détruis. Mais à la
fin du compte rien n'est perdu; le rouge que j'ai enlevé d'une
part se trouve quelque part ailleurs."[6]

Two things are pointed up by Stevens' use of this declaration
by Picasso. One is the aggressiveness of Stevens' posture in
"Blue Guitar": he translates *"somme"* as "hoard." In 1951, he
translated it "horde" (*NA*, 161), which suggests the direction of
his feelings. Against the horde of society he has his hoard of
destructions. The other thing pointed up by this passage is its
possibility as the source of the famous Stanza 22, Stevens' classic
description of poetry as a destructive force:

> Poetry is the subject of the poem,
> From this the poem issues and
>
> To this returns. Between the two,
> Between issue and return, there is
>
> An absence in reality,
> Things as they are. Or so we say.
>
> But are these separate? Is it
> An absence for the poem, which acquires
>
> Its true appearances there, sun's green,
> Cloud's red, earth feeling, sky that thinks?
>
> From these it takes. Perhaps it gives,
> In the universal intercourse.

Putting stanzas 15 and 22 together, there is no more explicit statement in all of Stevens' poetry of what might be called the self-sufficiency of reflection. The poet has only to look within himself to see society and to begin the destructive-creative process of poetry. He does not have to try to empathize with people who are unable to objectify, artistically, their feelings and their wishes. Those feelings and wishes are reflected in his own imagination and, more important, in a focused, or focusable, form.

Although it is not given great topical importance in the poem, war seems to figure imperatively in this focusing. Picasso used the word "*somme*" because he was speaking in 1935; Stevens used the word "hoard," suggesting "horde," because he was writing in 1936, after the Spanish Civil War had begun. The violence with which Stevens is finally able to resist the violence of the Depression is that of an imagination faced with the fact of war. Such a self is so much more sharply aware of its nothingness that the semi-nothingness of the sudden mobs of men in the Depression no longer seem a threat. For it seems to be a rule with Stevens that the more like a vacuum the self or the world becomes, the more it becomes pure force, pure destructiveness. This pure destructiveness is apparently what Picasso represented to Stevens. And yet the paradox contains a further paradox: the more destructive the self is, the more creative. This final paradox is, after all, the central meaning of the "rage for order" in "The Idea of Order at Key West": only when the self is completely chaotic, is it able to give birth to a complete cosmos.

The pressure for a socially conscious art during the Depression seemed to Stevens to be not a pressure for a completely new cosmos, but rather one in which only one thing was changed: the pay of the workers. Since it was not a thoroughgoing effort of the imagination, it was, in Stevens' view, a positive hindrance to the artist.

These matters—the pressure for a socially conscious art, usually in the name of Communism, and Picasso's independent artistic self-development—are brought together by Stevens in order to make just this point in his note about Williams in his essay "The Irrational Element":

> Williams is a writer to whom writing is the grinding of a glass, the polishing of a lens by means of which he hopes to be able to see clearly. His delineations are trials. They are rubbings of reality.
>
> The modern world is a result of such activity on a grand scale, not particularly in writing but in everything. It may be said, for instance, that communism is an effort to improve the human focus. The work of Picasso is an attempt to get at his subject, an attempt to achieve a reality of the intelligence.
>
> . . . .
>
> There is an intellectual *tenue*. It is easy to see how underneath the chaos of life today and at the bottom of all the disintegrations there is the need to see, to understand: and, in so far as one is not completely baffled, to recreate. This is not emotional. It springs from the belief that we have only our own intelligence on which to rely. This manifests in many ways, in every living art as in every living phase of politics or science. If we could suddenly re-make the world on the basis of our own intelligence, see it clearly and represent it without faintness or obscurity, Williams's poems would have a place there. (*OP*, 258-59)

In the light of what Stevens says of Communism elsewhere ("Communism is not the measure of humanity" in "Imagination as Value" [*NA*, 143]), Stevens clearly believed that it was a misguided effort to improve the human focus. But more important for our purpose is the juxtaposition of Picasso's attempt "to achieve a reality of the intelligence" and Stevens' belief that "we have only our own intelligence on which to rely" in our effort to see, to understand, and if possible to remake the world.

The end which Stevens tried to achieve "at the bottom of all the disintegrations"—that is, by means of his rejections—was a metamorphosis of reflection into refraction.

The other prose reference to Picasso and social pressure is less explicit but no less to the point:

> . . . the greater the pressure of the contemporaneous, the greater the resistance. Resistance is the opposite of escape. The poet who wishes to contemplate the good in the midst of confusion is like the mystic who wishes to contemplate God in the midst of evil. There can be no thought of escape. Both the poet and the mystic may establish themselves on herrings and apples. The painter may establish himself on a guitar, a copy of *Figaro* and a dish of melons. These are fortifyings, although irrational ones. The only possible resistance to the pressure of the contemporaneous is a matter of herrings and apples or, to be less definite, the contemporaneous itself. (*OP*, 225)

The refracting, focusing lens of the individual imagination composes the world in terms of the materials immediately at hand. If one of them happens to be one of the "fortifyings" or "Hoard of destructions" provided by a kindred artist—say, a guitar in a Picasso still life—it will do. If the guitar should seem poor and pale (Stanza 20) for the great task imposed on it—that of taking the place of empty heaven (Stanza 5)—it can still do it. Its focusing blue color can turn into the blue of the jay, which because it is an undreaming felon brings heaven down to earth.

IV   "A Thought Revolved"

In the two poems which Stevens placed immediately after "Blue Guitar" "A Thought Revolved" and "The Men That Are Falling," there is an unusually candid and revitalized loathing for people who are incapable of either reflection or refraction. N. P. Stallknecht has said: "Stevens would seem to lack Coleridge's sympathy, expressed in 'Dejection,' for those who live without benefits of imagination. His attitude toward the 'mickey mockers' is less generous than Coleridge's feeling for the 'poor loveless ever-anxious crowd.'"[7] Stallknecht might have used the last line of "The Mechanical Optimist" (the first section of "A Thought Revoived"): "Dying lady, rejoice, rejoice!" which may be reasonably suspected of being an ironical echo of the last two lines of "Dejection": "Dear Lady! friend devoutest of my choice,/ Thus mayest thou ever, evermore rejoice." Coleridge tries vainly to find in his own depressed state of mind something to revive his "shaping spirit of imagination" in order to cheer up the lady to whom the poem is addressed, who apparently needs gentle sleep's "wings of healing" and the "beauty-making power" of joy, and who shares with Coleridge (and with "the poor loveless ever-anxious crowd") "Reality's dark dream."

The lady whom Stevens addresses may be poor and loveless, but she is never anxious; in fact, she might be said to be dying in her spirit because the life of her fancy (as opposed to her imagination, in Coleridge's terms) is too sweet, just as her body is dying of diabetes.

This poem is unquestionably Stevens' most savage satire on vulgarity, and it is noteworthy that it is not specifically working-class vulgarity. Stevens' Depression experience, concentrated and redeemed in "Blue Guitar," confirmed him once and for all in his own particular form of neo-romanticism—one that is quite explicit about its belief that the present day "poet and painter alike live and work in the midst of a generation that is experiencing essential poverty in spite of fortune," (NA, 17), but one equally explicit that the poverty is one of mythology.

It is at this point that Stevens starts the hard work on the hero of his later poetry. All the ingredients are present in "Blue Guitar": the apparent absurdity of the blueness in the first part (stanzas 1-10) and the real absurdity of the Hoon-like idealism in the second part (stanzas 11-20) are transmuted into confidence in a creative-destructive world-self in the third part (stanzas 21-30). This world-self makes the strange unlike of the blueness in Part I simply one of the things that the poetic *mundo* takes from the physical world and then gives back. This world-self also makes the Hoon-like idealism of Part II into an identity between the poetic *mundo* and the physical world. Now all that remains—and it is a staggering task—is to give this transfigured strangeness and idealism a believable human form.

"Mystic Garden & Middling Beast," the second part of "A Thought Revolved," rehearses the obvious impediments to this task: the American vulgar. For all the poet's seeking for "peaks outsoaring possible adjectives," he is not striding among the stars but among "cigar stores," "Ryan's lunch," rather than Orion's hunt; "hatters" who keep the sky out of most people's lives; "insurance and medicines" that postpone the prospect of death and the purpose of life. All that is left of the poet is an idea of his struggling with the idea of the best in man in a renewed image of "the mystic garden and the middling beast." "God" is uncapitalized, so that the last line, "And he that created the garden and peopled it," is probably deliberately ambiguous. Stevens says in the essay "Two or Three Ideas" that the true creators and sustainers of religious belief are not the priests but the poets who make the gods real to the people (*OP*, 208). In the terms of this poem, the poet primarily essays to make a man ideal to himself, without naming a particular god, as Virgil did, Aeneas being the son of Venus; and thus the writer avoids providing mechanical optimists with fixities and definites, like Dido, for them to identify with. Instead, the poet feels himself to be a part of a "universe of reproduction," which is not "an assembly line but an incessant creation" (*NA*, 73). Thus his "peaks outsoaring possible adjectives," on which he hears "hero hymns,/Chorals for mountain voices," are, to begin with, skyscrapers rising from "his infernal walls," his "space of stone, of inexplicable base." And the hymns he hears on those heroic heights are of the struggle of the idea of God and the idea of man. With a heroic effort he transfigures the ordinariness that is an opiate for the unimaginative.

In "Romanesque Affabulation," the third section of "A Thought Revolved," affabulation is an act of making something legendary. Although the poet has dropped "the cloak and speech of Virgil," his purpose is still Virgilian and hence romanesque: to make a down-to-earth hero in the light of the ideal or godlike. One can see now that "A Thought Revolved" follows a parabolic course: it rises out of the mechanical hell of the living dead (the lady dying of diabetes), up the mountain of purgatory (leaving Virgil behind) to the garden of earthly paradise at its top, and now down again to hell, bringing the image of an ideal leader, looking for one of the living dead in whom to educe that image.

In "The Leader," the fourth and last part of "A Thought Revolved," the man the poet finds who comes closest to fulfilling these attributes looks like Stevens' pejorative notion of a Marxian revolutionist. His whore, "Morning Star," is not Venus; and she has not the ideal relationship to him that Venus had to Aeneas.

She is dressed like the lady in "The Mechanical Optimist" and wears an overpoweringly sweet-smelling flower, the syringa, along with "his flea" in her hair. Morning Star, instead of being the divine guide and support of the leader's manhood, is the soft, sweet hope on which he battens like a flea. Thus this leader is not "The faster's feast and heavy-fruited star" of "Romanesque Affabulation," but the opposite: he is indistinguishable from the barefoot beggars.

Attached as the leader is to a sentimental, materialistic hope, like the one that Stevens believed to be that of Communism, he is not up against the hard barrier of reality that would make him "Shelter yet thrower of the summer spear." On the contrary, his salient points are his great toe, which probably signifies his material poverty and his spiritual inertness (he is not even "striding among the cigar stores"), and his nose, which may suggest both his "knows" and his "nose," since it grew "thin and taut" (taught) from reading "In how severe a book" that dropped its poisonous knowledge upon his heart "half the night." That is, not only is Venus degraded to a whore, but the leader is so bookish and thought-bound that it would be inconceivable for him to be "He that at midnight touches the guitar." He is out of touch with both the ideal and the real. Thus his dreams of Roman grandeur,

> the nobler works of man,
> The gold facade round early squares,
> The bronzes liquid through gay light.

are "minor wish-fulfillments" (*NA*, 139: Stevens' phrase for the achievement of the romantic in the bad sense). It is a scholarly, absent-minded, remote kind of fantasy: "He hummed to himself at such a plan."

In summary, the earthly leader most likely to fulfill the requirement of the ideal leader is so out of touch with the vital ideal and with the hard reality that, even when he stubs his toe on the material poverty with which he allies himself, he cannot feel it. In the light of the morning sun (not the Morning Star), such a calloused sensibility is not a horn of strength but "The central flaw." That is, he is no more inclined to seek the *high* bareness—the "essential poverty"—of the Alps than is the mechanical optimist; and so the thought has revolved full circle. In fact, the circle is likely to continue to turn again on itself; for Morning Star, more than the leader, resembles the lady in "The Mechanical Optimist." If his revolution were successful, the leader would probably produce a *Lumpenproletariat* as comfortable and as secure from any real confrontation with death and life as that dying lady.

V   "The Men That Are Falling"

In this poem, it is not the men who are rising that keep the poet awake with desire and dark dreaming; it is the men who are falling. It is not the labor movement, for instance—which he regarded as "in the main, a revolution for more pay" (*NA*, 19)— but "the collapse of our system" (*NA*, 20) or the "war-like whole" (*NA*, 31). Whoever dies for his love of earth—even if that love is called Communism—has faced the ultimate reality of death for it. Benamou points out that this poem appeared at a time (a few months after the beginning of the Spanish Civil War) and in a place (*The Nation*) that makes it evidently a poem about a Spanish revolutionary.[8] Heaven—God and all angels—has sung everyone else to sleep; and the meaning of life utters itself to the poet as if from the head of a martyr on his pillow—one of the "lost remembrances" on which "the moon/Burns in the mind." The meaning of life is "the immaculate syllables/That he spoke only by doing what he did" because he "loved earth . . . enough to die." The poet too has suffered that death, though he loses his remembrance of it in work and in sleep; for the poet too has felt the pressure of the contemporaneous, the war-like whole, and the collapse of our system. The poet has not sought to profit, either in pay or power, from the collapse; and so he can cry out against those who have: pensioners, demagogues, and pay-men.

In the light of the discussion of "Blue Guitar" and of "A Thought Revolved," "The Men That Are Falling" emphasizes the focusing effect of actual death; and it asserts that the only real heroes of "the war-like whole" are those who die in the struggle. It thereby prefigures the effect of the war, which focused the interests and energies of the whole Western world on "the collapse of our system," concretely imaged in the death of the young men who would sustain it if they were not dying for it. If "The Men That Are Falling" is indeed about a Spanish revolutionary, it is even more clearly a prefiguration of the effect of World War II. As one historian said in 1955, the Spanish Civil War "is still a kind of great collective Dreyfus case, a test of conscience and loyalty for our time."[9]

VI   Parts of a World

Ideas of Order expresses a rather desperate ambivalence and frustration which is not resolved until "Blue Guitar" clearly declares the self-sufficiency of the poet's individual reflection. *Parts of a World* therefore has a more definite modus from the outset, a greater confidence in the poet's right to pursue his sensibility wherever it may lead him. And with the war-hero poems at the end as a positive goal in relation to which Stevens could arrange the rest of the poems, it is no wonder the book as a whole falls into a neater and more significant order than did *Ideas of Order*. The very title suggests that these poems constitute parts of a single world, rather than several ideas of order.

Parts of a World begins with a series of poems—from "Parochial Theme" to "The Latest Freed Man"—which reject the rational will that makes the fixed or mechanical orders that frustrate the poet in the Depression poems. This will is best represented, among the poems I have already discussed, by "The Leader" in "A Thought Revolved." Then, in the second series of poems in *Parts of a World*, from "United Dames of America" to "The Sense of the Sleight-of-Hand Man," the poet makes the necessary next step after the rejection: the confrontation with bare sense experience; and for this he becomes an ignorant man again. In the third series of poems, from "The Candle a Saint" to "Yellow Afternoon," the emphasis is on a confrontation with *all* the senses, not just the anaesthetized eyesight of those who have not become ignorant men again. In the fourth series of poems—from "Martial Cadenza" to "Arrival at the Waldorf"—the war clearly appears, and with it a new acceptance of men in a wintry slime ("Arrival at the Waldorf" is a more cheerful version of "Farewell to Florida") *and* at war; for in war their energies and feelings are brought to a focus (refraction), much like the focus of all the senses emphasized in the preceding series of poems. (This part roughly parallels the first part of *Ideas of Order*.) Then in the fifth series of poems, from "Landscape with Boat" to "Mrs. Alfred Uruguay," the poet dismisses the assumption that there is another world beyond this one of the senses; for, if one assumes such an Other World, one can never accept bare sense experience as the final refracting medium. This part is roughly parallel to the second part of *Ideas of Order*—the part dealing with organized religion. Finally, sixth, at the end of *Parts of a World*, there is a group of poems devoted entirely to the hero: from "Asides on the Oboe" to "Examination of the Hero in a Time of War."

The twelve poems from "Parochial Theme" to "The Latest Freed Man" can be divided into three groups. The first two poems—the second is "Poetry Is a Destructive Force"—serve as an introduction, making first an abortive return to nature and then an alliance with the destructive element in nature, thus getting the poet back to the situation he was in at the end of "Like Decorations in a Nigger Cemetery." "The Poems of Our Climate," "Prelude to Objects," "Study of Two Pears," "The Glass of Water," and "Add This to Rhetoric"—the next five poems—are still lifes, quite possibly inspired by Picasso, since the first genuine still life in Stevens' poetry occurs in "Blue Guitar" in connection with the Picasso quote. Stevens believed that both the poet and the painter, in their "resistance to the pressure of the contemporaneous," must establish themselves on "herrings and apple"—on "the contemporaneous itself" (*OP*, 225). And by that Stevens meant whatever came closest to hand: the flowers and fruits he enjoyed in the very room in which he wrote. Thus Stevens in these five poems goes ahead with the program he decided on in "Blue Guitar": that of working out the destiny of his imagination and his art without trying to identify his consciousness in any way with that of the oppressed masses of the Depression. The problem he works on in these poems is that of the limits of the rational will, rather constantly symbolized by efforts to rationally "pose" things with the hands.

In the next five poems—"Dry Loaf," "Idiom of the Hero," "The Man on the Dump," "On the Road Home," and "The Latest Freed Man"—the poet turns again to landscape and, in the last poem, to the interior of a house—his more characteristic settings. Taking the lesson of the first five poems to heart, the poet virtually rejects the rational will altogether, never losing sight of the fact that, implicitly, the will must be there first in order for its rejection to have the fecundating effect that he prizes. That is, he never sets out to write a poem without beginning with a representation of a rational will. The culminating symbol of the faculty that takes the place of the rational will is the eye: the intuition. This hand-eye conflict develops throughout *Parts of a World*: the hand tends to analyze and assemble parts; the eye, to create and discover the whole world. (But in the third series the eye is rejected, in favor of all the senses, as the medium through which the self confronts the whole world.)

This traditional romantic conflict between the mechanical and the organic was announced as a problem to receive special attention in "A Thought Revolved," although it had a central role in "Like Decorations in a Nigger Cemetery," "Owl's Clover," and "Blue Guitar." But the emphasis, especially in "Owl's Clover" and in "Blue Guitar," was on the combination of mechanism and sentimentality in social beliefs. In *Parts of a World*, with the concentration of a Picasso-like interest in simple perception, a central romantic *artistic* problem is examined. The poet is at last freely "practicing arpeggios" and is decidedly out of the dilemma he was in in "Mozart, 1935." He has found an order, however small.

The order is, nevertheless, a noble one. In "Poetry Is a Destructive Force," for instance, one is not merely "a man/In the body of a violent beast" but a man in the king of beasts. One is in a position to impose, majestically, a new order, even if it looks like chaos and even if it depends on the extinction of the human self as it has hitherto been defined: that is, as a function of the rational will.

Thus, soon after the beginning of *Parts of a World*, one finds himself in the same position he was in at the end of "Like Decorations in a Nigger Cemetery" but without its black despair. A tone of grim determination in *Parts of a World* arises from the decision taken in "Blue Guitar": to follow one's individual sensibility wherever it may lead. If it leads to a life of a nose on paws, limited as this may seem, it is not the life of ponies of Parisians "nosing the pine-lands," a domesticated, led-by-the-nose kind of back-to-nature movement. And it is certainly not the life of "The Leader," whose "nose grew thin and taut/And knowledge dropped upon his heart/Its pitting poison half the night"—a heart full of the bitterness and frustration of knowing too much.

If one must become an ignorant man again, one must do so.

Thus "The imperfect is our paradise." And it is "so hot in us" that "delight . . . Lies in flawed words and stubborn sounds." This is the conclusion of "Poems of Our Climate": a composition in words—unlike one that one makes with one's hands—contains, even when delightful, both an intellectual and a sensuous sense of the conflict with chaos which enrages and engages the whole man. The will for order, the reason, is finally irrational: what finally satisfies it is not order but an encounter with its own chaotic origin. One may presume that this chaotic origin is paradise because it is actually an order so primordial that it is no longer intelligible to men, who are able and inclined to simplify their days with bowls of flowers.

"Prelude to Objects" adds that in poetry one can only touch the world; one cannot take it apart and put it together again as in natural science. Therefore, the science that grows out of present poetry will be one of perception; and present poetry is a pre-scientific discipline of perception. This discipline insists that the black, irregular self that is concealed by the egocentric predicament must be brought into a position of public authority. Thus the poet avoids "patting more nonsense/Foamed from the sea": that is, he gets out of the Louvre or the S.S. *Normandie* and its now-prefabricated myths like that of Venus, who arose from the sea-foam. Of course, what he fabricates also has an element of nonsense in it; it is a more or less deliberate illusion that he creates to fortify himself against chaos; but it is an illusion that, according to Stevens, is justified by his stark need for order and verdure when he confronts the hardness or the nothingness or the chaos of reality. And it is an illusion that is scrupulously designed to sharpen and enlighten perception.

"Study of Two Pears" is probably as rigorous a study of perception as any that Stevens ever made. Each word is self-consciously used as a shaping tool or a clarifying lens in a dialectic of sensation and form. Stevens excuses the perspicacity of the piece with the first two words, "Opusculum paedagogum." He is saying that he knows this is elementary and in a sense pedantic, but that it pretends to be only a little lesson. Then the arpeggios begin.

The next three lines reject the Louvre-like reflected projections, taking examples from music, painting, and the art of living

—viols, nudes, or bottles. In Stanza II, each phrase contains two principle terms: one, a term for a sensation; the other, for an aspect of form. These combinations alternate the order of the terms: "yellow forms" (sense, form), "composed of curves" (form, sense), "Bulging toward the base" (sense, form), "touched red" (form, sense). Taken as a continuous description, the series of phrases as a whole moves from sense to form to sense to form to sense. The whole series also moves from a term for a paler sensation and a more abstract one for form to a quite concrete one for form (the act of touching giving "touched" most of its significance) and to a more intense sensation.

The over-all import of the series is that, as one imagines a forming action—sculpting and painting—as the cause of the form and color of the object, one's perception of the object becomes more and more precise and vivid. "Forms composed," as a suggestion of such a forming action, forces the object to assert its own form, virtually as a kind of resistance to that forming action, with "curves bulging." But as the curves bulge they indicate a direction and an end, an aspect of form achieved by a convergence of the object's resistance to the forming action and one of the ends of the forming action: "the base." Thus the last, most concrete conjunction of the forming action and resisting sensation is also the closest conjunction. The form of the red and the red of the form are practically indistinguishable: it is as if the painter has only barely to touch the object with his red brush to make the red in the object leap up to meet the brush. Thus, although the first word in the sequence is a sense word, other and finer sense words are called out only by other and finer form words.

Stanza III is a reaction, on the part of the poet, to the mounting forming action, especially its painter-like character of Stanza II. "They are not flat surfaces," not paintings of pears. "Having curved outlines": "curved outlines" sums up the whole sequence of actions and reactions in "Composed of curves/Bulging toward the base." "They are round": "round" is a comparatively abstract sense word. The object asserts its own form in a more serene way than it did in Stanza II with "bulging" and "red." "Tapering" continues this serener self-assertion of the object. This time both the object's assertion of its sense and the forming action meeting that assertion are in a gentler accord. The over-all effect of Stanza III is that of taking off the pressure of the forming action in

Stanza II and thus taming the action of the object. Whereas the object was "touched red" at the end of II, as with the point of a sword in a duel, the object at the end of III comes "tapering toward the top," as to a lump of sugar.

Because of the harmony between the poet's forming action and the object's self-assertion at the end of III, the poet begins Stanza IV with a bold, explicit forming action: "In the way that they are modelled." This action accentuates the sculptural quality of the object and also suggests that it is made in imitation of something else. The line, "There are bits of blue," as a reaction to this forming action, may even contribute to this sense of imitation; for blue in Stevens is a fairly constant symbol of the ideal or the imagined. And since the poem insists on presenting the real pears, rather than images of them, the only other pears they could be modelled after would be ideal pears. Whether "modelled" and "blue" carry this particular connotation or not, "way" and "modelled," simply by their explicitness, bring the object to an equal explicitness of sensuous response: "bits of blue." "Bits of blue" is, in its own way, as quick a response as "touched red"; only it is more independent, like a tiny spontaneous explosion. In this mood of spontaneity, and perhaps in reaction to the ideality suggested by "modelled" and "blue," the pears make a small but audacious declaration of independence of all forming action: "A hard dry leaf hangs/From the stem." In Stanza V, the object is so released from the restraint of forming actions that it first "glistens," and then its glistening proliferates into "various yellows"; and these, by their names, suggest what are literally organic metaphors, "Citrons, oranges and greens." The object has asserted not only its own form but has born its own fruitful resemblances, "Flowering over the skin."

In Stanza VI the poet makes one last effort to capture or domesticate the object, by observing its "shadows . . . on the green cloth." In its shadows the object would have to obey the light, which, considering the situation, might be domesticated by a window and a room; and it would also have to adapt itself to the controlled texture of the green cloth. But the pears triumph over this domesitication; their shadows are "blobs" on the green cloth. The last two lines simply report the formal surrender of the forming forces, the rational will of the observer: "The pears are not seen/As the observer wills."

Thus, in direct proportion to the effort to impose form on an object, the object successfully defeats that effort. And as I have noted in "The Poems of Our Climate" and in "Prelude to Objects," the poet takes a bitter delight not in dominating reality with his rational will but in so pressing reality with his will that reality fights back and defeats it. Perception, as the power to let things speak for themselves, is sharpened and clarified by an intermittent forming action, training the object to become self-determining.

"Prelude to Objects" brought the problem of perceiving the external world to a focus with the command, "Design the touch"; and "Study of Two Pears" carried out that command. But "The Glass of Water" considers the problem in a more theoretical way, and in this broader context looks again into the outside world, even into the world of politics. But even the world of politics is represented in a way that makes it another still life, susceptible of the same kind of technical and theortical examination that the two pears and the glass of water are susceptible of.

"The Glass of Water" begins with the assertion that there is a correspondence between the physical and the metaphysical states of the object. Then it asserts that there is a correspondence between the metaphysical state of the object and the state of mind of the observer, and thereby introduces a correspondence between a state of mind and a state of society. The entire poem can be read as an elaborate series of puns on the word "state."

The predators of society, the politicians, have their own form of abstract meditation, card-playing. The poet is not alone in his concentration on "herrings and apples" or "arpeggios"; for the very people who most concern themselves with the life that the poet is said to be escaping escape it in much the same way, and for much the same purpose—that of coming to closer grips with its metaphysical and psychological essences.

"The Glass of Water" ends with a tension between the two verbs "discover" and "contend," which go with the problem of unwinding the "winding weeds" in the metaphysical idea of the self and the corresponding problem of resisting the crash of *metaphysica* within the mind. This outer-inner metaphor has been central to all the still-lifes, having been introduced by the inner beast which becomes the engorging outer body of the poet in "Poetry is a Destructive Force."

In "Add This to Rhetoric" the inner-outer metaphor is given what is, for the moment, a final, more explicit statement by showing how the actual, achieved poses of objects either fall or vanish into thin air; but the sense that creates these poses responds and corresponds to the sun, which "For all your images,/ Comes up as the sun, bull fire." Behind any object, and before any posing of that object by speech or by paint or by music, burns a Heraclitean fire; and it is in it that the object, as an image or a pose, "moves and speaks." "This is the figure and not/An evading metaphor" because it includes the image of the object, the human impulse that creates that image, and the force in reality or nature of which the human impulse is an expression. The perceiver hotly presses against the image with his imagination—in Santayana's sense of "the self-consciousness of instinct"[10] —and reality, the sun, also presses hotly against the image, from the other side, so to speak. Thus hotly held, the object "moves and speaks"; it does not drop to sleep like a beggar or vanish like a puff of cloud; and it is "the figure" and not an image that seeks to evade the interaction of sun and sense, reality and the imagination. "The figure" that "moves and speaks" in the merged fires of sun and sense is an addition of reality, both human and natural, to rhetoric. As such, it is a real addition.

"Dry Loaf"—with its careful correspondences ("It is equal to living in a tragic land/To live in a tragic time") and its suggestion that a landscape is similar to a still-life ("That was what I painted behind the loaf")—could be read as a still life like "Prelude to Objects" or "The Glass of Water." The reason "Dry Loaf" fits better with the four poems that follow it than it does with the five that precede it is that it is concerned with expanding circles of significance rather than with an in-focusing of significance, as in the still lifes. "Dry Loaf," along with the rest of the first eleven poems in *Parts of a World*, was first published in the autumn of 1938; and the wider significance of "it was the hungry that cried/And the waves, the waves were soldiers moving" probably included not only the Depression and the Spanish Civil war but the *Anschluss*. "Prelude to Objects" ends with the line, "We are conceived in your conceits," speaking of a conception that designs the touch and fixes quiet and thus *concentrates* general human powers. "The Glass of Water" ends with the sentence, "Among the dogs and dung,/One would continue to contend with one's ideas" and prepares for the bringing of the world of politics into the perceptual concentration of "Prelude to Objects." But "Dry Loaf" ends with the sentence, "No doubt that soldiers had to be marching/and that drums had to be rolling, rolling, rolling." These lines permanently liquify the poet's original concentration on the mountain rock as on a loaf of bread and lets it spread outward without limit.

"Dry Loaf" benefits from the lessons of the five preceding poems primarily in its reliance on the discipline of the still-life painter as the point of concentration from which endless waves of significance can emanate. And the significance of what the poet paints behind the loaf is the insignificance of his efforts to pose and contain the objects of his disciplined perception: they all roll away, endlessly. They obey currents of seasonal and historical hunger that are far beyond his rational control.

Furthermore, the image of a dirty un-nourishing loaf, made out of rocks, is a continuation of the image at the end of "Blue Guitar": "Here is the bread of time to come,/Here is its actual stone"—and of its Stanza XVI: "The earth is not earth but a stone." In the last stanza of "Blue Guitar," the bread appears as part of a liquid element: imagination.

In the context of world-wide currents of hunger and war, the poet returns briefly in "Idiom of the Hero" to the theme of "Like Decorations in a Nigger Cemetery," "Owl's Clover," and "Blue Guitar," which can be summarized in a sentence in the last stanza of the "Like Decorations": "Union of the weakest develops strength/Not wisdom." The ordinary practical men of the world, the workers, suppose that the rational will can triumph over universal hunger and war. The six preceding poems show that this supposition is not a part of wisdom; "Idiom of the Hero" indicates that it is also not a part of valor. The last stanza in "Like Decorations in a Nigger Cemetery" concludes, ". . . the wise man avenges by building his city in snow": he befriends the destructive element. In "Idiom of the Hero" the destructive element is entirely human; and the wise hero looks up from that human poverty and chaos to "the blue house," "the clouds, pomp of the air," not for therapeutic attention ("not to be attended" and "mended") but for the friendship that opposing warriors instinctively feel for each other.

Thus in "Idiom of the Hero" the poet has come full circle

from his position in "Poetry is a Destructive Force," in which the poet found that out of his inner poverty and misery grows a beast that in the end encloses him. This discovery grew out of the poet's obedience to his own command at the end of the preceding poem, "Parochial Theme:" "Piece the world together, boys, but not with your hands." If a rational manipulation of the world will not work, then one must look into one's heart. Thus, the inner-outer metaphor of the beastly imagination can be interpreted to apply particularly to the limits of reason; and the five still lifes that follow "Poetry is a Destructive Force" study the limits of rational control on an external object and show that it only prods the object into expressing its own beastly instincts.

The external object of these studies is an analogue of the self; and, as the irrational forces within the object show themselves more and more to be the regnant reality, the surprise and terror in "Poetry is a Destructive Force" at the discovery that the self is, at heart, irrational is gradually replaced by an acceptance of that irrationality. In "Idiom of the Hero" the poet speaks from the point of view of that irrationality and looks up to the ideals of reason as to a friendly enemy. Having done all he can with his hands in the still lifes, he can bluntly contradict the wishful thinking of the workers rather than satirize that thinking—as he does in "Parochial Theme," "A Thought Revolved," and "Blue Guitar."

He is now in a position not only to establish himself on herrings and apples; he can speak directly from the irrational forces within himself that correspond with those within the objects of his perception: his hunger, as in "Dry Loaf"; or his poverty, as in "Idiom of the Hero." He no longer looks on his task as that of rationally trying to control his perceptions in order to make them fecundate from within; he now sees his task as that of letting himself respond instinctively, heroically, to his essential poverty and of recognizing the cloudy ideals of reason as his friendly and necessary enemy. As a hero, he is an object of perception, like the two pears; and he is at war with the reason that tries to contain him, just as in "Study of Two Pears," the pears were at war with his reason—his efforts rationally to contain them in forms.

"The Man on the Dump," making explicit the rejection of old containing images—even images of freshness, like "dew"—permits one to see a thing without an image of it. One can do this only when *on* the dump: when one is clearly aware of all the made or cultivated things and flowers, decorative metaphors, that one has rejected. Only in that explicit poverty and misery do objects come to the senses purified of all their entanglements and encasements in images, words, and categories; and only then is one a man who is similarly purified.

To beat an "old tin can, lard pail" is to realize that one's emptiness has no solacing ring or roll (a lard pail does not resonate), and thus one can avoid the hypnotized feeling of necessity that the poet got from the battering of drums in "Dry Loaf," as well as, of course, the false feeling of a cleansing return to nature that the Parisians got in "Parochial Theme"—ignoring as they did "the rattle of sticks/On tins and boxes," the mechanical character of their return to nature. But, if beating a lard pail avoids at least two kinds of romantic illusion, what does it offer in their place? It is no surprise that the poet, in the light of "Idiom of the Hero," answers "merely oneself."

Suppose one calls the explicitness of being on the dump in spring, *aptest eve*; suppose one's beating the lard pail evokes the blatter of the anti-romantic anti-nightingale, the grackle or the crow, an *invisible priest* that mediates between the hungry disgust of the imaginative self and the disgusting hunger of reality. And suppose that with the help of the purgating explicitness provided by *aptest eve* and the contact with reality provided by *invisible priest* one can actually analyze one's experience into its real parts and can make of the stanza that bodies forth that analysis and that realization the foundation stone for one's belief ("to eject, to pull/The day to pieces and cry *stanza my stone*"). Where is there in all this purgating, making contact, and analyzing any news of the truth? Since all of these absolute experiences occur in an unplanned, evanescent, infinitely repeatable and infinitely variable way, none of them can be said to be the only one of its kind. None of them can be contained by the definite article "the." The poet cannot say "*the aptest eve, the invisible priest, the stanza my stone.*" If the truth is single, these are not the truth, even though they occur as a result of one's pursuing the truth. Thus "The Man on the Dump" can end only ambiguously: "Where was it one first heard of the truth? The the." One answer to that question—and, in the light of "Idiom of the

Hero," a likely one—would be "In the singularity of the self." But, since the self is essentially irrational, this would be to say that the single self's pursuit of a single truth is motivated by a metaphysical hunger as instinctive and irrational as physical hunger, a misery of man without god that is one with "the misery of a man on a dump." Therefore, "that which one believes" and for which "one beats and beats" is possibly "merely oneself."

Another possible answer to the question at the end of "The Man on the Dump" is "There is no such thing as the truth," the second line in "On the Road Home," which follows "The Man on the Dump." To see the world without feeling the need to unify it under one grand abstraction is to see it more fecund and to see it responding to that increased fecundity, as the fox responds to the fatter grapes.

The poet is walking with someone on the road home. The two have the same destination, which is essentially themselves. They both see the same things, only each a little differently. "You" responds to the fattening of the grapes and the appetite of the fox by saying " 'There are many truths,/But they are not parts of a truth.' " That is, each particular of perception has its own "truth of fact" (in "The Figure of the Youth as Virile Poet," *NA*, 59); but these truths do not fit together logically, once and for all into a system that can be summed up with *a* truth. The new wholes created between or beneath the ticks of time change too fast to be held in a logical consistency. When "you" say this, the tree begins to diffuse its half-colors in the night; its "smoking" makes its form infinitely changeable. It no longer has the distinct parts-to-whole interrelationships and symmetry of branches and trunk. In a world thus becoming indistinct, "I" and "you" become the only things that can be distinguished from each other and from the rest of the world. Like "figures in a wood," which might be a painting, they become aware of the mere perceptibleness of themselves and thus of their being susceptible of being merely denoted by words: "We said we stood alone."

The shift from thought, with its concern for "truth" or "truths," to perception, with its concern with what is "said," is made explicit in what "I" now says: "Words are not forms of a single word./In the sum of the parts, there are only the parts./The world must be measured by eye." "Words" take the place of "truths," and then "eye" takes the place of "words." Words have the same bad effect on perception that truths have: they divide up experience so that it cannot be reunited into a whole again. They are too rigid; they change too little to be continuously accurate in sizing up the world. Only the eye has the requisite flexibility. Then, before the world can respond to this new definition of perception, "you" says, "The idols have seen lots of poverty,/Snakes and gold and lice,/But not the truth."

Either "the truth" or "truths" or "words" or "a single word" go with "figures in a wood": definite, fixed "idols" or images of the self. It is out of deference to a fixed, definite conception of one's self that one uses fixed and definite concepts of other things. As one conceives the self, so one conceives the world. Thus all that an idol-like self, composed of words, can measure with its eye are aspects of the world that resemble itself: the vermin and the money that are left when a society's growth has been cut off by a fixed definition of it and there is no more natural wealth that can be bought with the money. Idols see only the essential poverty of "the gaunt world of the reason," to use another phrase from "The Figure of the Youth as Virile Poet" (*NA*, 58). The passage in which it occurs is appropriate here: "It is the *mundo* of the imagination in which the imaginative man delights and not the gaunt world of the reason. The pleasure is the pleasure of powers that create a truth that cannot be arrived at by the reason alone, a truth that the poet recognizes by sensation. The morality of the poet's radiant and productive atmosphere is the morality of the right sensation" (*NA*, 57-58). "The truth that the poet recognizes by sensation" is not a truth that he gets parasitically, sucking the juice out of it as lice do or taking abstract measures of its wealth, like gold, as idols do. The "morality of the right sensation" seeks "a pleasure of agreement with the radiant and productive world" (*NA*, 57), not the predatory gratification of a snake, which is traditionally alien and at odds with the rest of creation.

When "I" and "you" together discard the self that is an idol made of words,

> It was at that time, that the silence was largest
> And longest, the night was roundest,
> The fragrance of the autumn warmest,
> Closest and strongest.

All the adjectives are now superlatives, but the absolute agreement between the world and the homeward-bound poet and friend is not an absolutely determining truth but one that results from an escape from all determination—a surrender to pure sensation. "I" and "you" have arrived at their home: the world around them agrees with them.

"The Latest Freed Man" concludes the first sequence of poems in *Parts of a World* simply by stating Stevens' positive belief as plainly and unambiguously as possible. The world without a doctrine or a description is only sensible particulars—"the moment's rain and sea,/The moment's sun (the strong man vaguely seen)"—and the self that responds to the sun which "bathes in the mist/Like a man without a doctrine" becomes an ox, strong like an ox, and of a bulk that defies accurate description, like an ox. (Stevens may be playing, also, on the resemblance of "ox" to "x.")

Now that the essentially irrational and sensuous character of Stevens' artistic self is clearly established, the reader can proceed more quickly through the rest of the poems in *Parts of a World*. In "United Dames of America" this irrational, sensuous character is expressed in an image of nakedness. The latest freed man—"The actor that will at last declaim our end"—is so naked (so alive, so sensitive, so opposite to "the man/Of this dead mass") that there are not enough leaves to crown or cover him. He is like the prophet Daniel in "Country Words" (he also figured in the story of Susanna and the Elders), telling Belshazzar, not of the decay of his kingdom, but "Of being, more than birth or death." Country words might also describe the willful decay of the self which is entirely the mind, "The Dwarf," when it finds itself in a cocoon made out of the used-up thoughts of summer. Or, in the equivalent condition of night, it may be "A Rabbit as King of the Ghosts"; that is, it may go to the other extreme of false self-apotheosis. This is the opposite of Hoon's all-inclusiveness because it is made out of darkness rather than light. It is as if the submam at the end of "Owl's Clover" mistook the sprawling portent that grows out of him for a good omen. Or it is like the false confidence of "the Polacks" that "pass in their motors/And play concertinas all night," in "Loneliness in Jersey City;" "*They* think that things are all right,/Since the deer and the dachshund are one."

The effect of this vulgar kind of confidence upon the artist is only to increase his loneliness. He is like a visiting colonial, "The Johannisberger, Hans" in "Anything Is Beautiful if You Say It Is": he is capable of loving "the window's lemon light,/The very will of the nerves,/The crack across the pane,/The dirt along the sill." But the kept women of society are limited to either anathematizing the place or saying "Hey-de-i-do!"—a verbal gesture that suggests both throwing up one's hands and kicking up one's heels.

The poet is, however, more at home as "A Weak Mind in the Mountains," where the winds destroy his mind. Then, unable to weave any kind of protection, the mental self is annihilated: "there was a man within me/Could have risen to the clouds,/Could have touched these winds,/Bent and broken them down,/Could have stood up sharply in the sky." The rational will that the poet has escaped also has a more violent, malignant character than the images of the cocoon and of the kept women suggest. In "The Bagatelles the Madrigals" it takes the form of a snake in hibernation. In "Girl in a Nightgown" it is the "Massive drums and leaden trumpets,/Perceived by feeling instead of sense."

The girl in the nightgown is the small, helpless capacity to feel that is expressed in "Connoisseur of Chaos" by the image of the identity of the opposites, order and chaos, being not like "statuary, posed" but "things chalked/On the sidewalk so that the pensive men may see." That is, the underlying conflict that is generally the subject matter of these poems—namely, the inexorable pursuit of the purely sensuous, emotional artist by the rational will he has rejected—is not a conflict for the artist in his most innocent aspect. It is rather like a child's game—hopscotch —that only a pensive man would take solemnly, and then only because in his habitual solemnity he is always looking at the ground.

Or this small helpless capacity to feel is like the mouse in "The Blue Buildings in the Summer Air," which Cotton Mather can neither explain away nor ignore in his efforts to bring his Byzantine heaven down to wooden Boston. This mouse is told to "go nibble at Lenin in his tomb," since Lenin tried to lift the earth up to heaven or—to put it more in accord with Stevens' opinion of Communism—to make a wooden heaven out of Russia's Byzantine. This mouse not only destroys idle dreams of glories invented and imposed by the rational will; it also hunts for the true honeycomb of the heart's desire. "Dezembrum" puts it quite plainly: "The reason can give nothing at all/Like the response to desire." And Stevens has no juicier display of what he means by "the response to desire" than "Poem Written at Morning." In it, for a moment at least, the senses bring forth their giant without strain or defensive aggression.

But the reader is back in the war with pseudo-heroics in the next poem, "Thunder by the Musician." The situation in it is much like that of Basilewski's abortive concerto in · "Owl's Clover," only this time the trouble is not with the music as a bubble, or here, a diamond, but with the character of the man that is represented as holding the diamond. Stevens' point is, as usual, that only if the man confesses his weakness is he able to find his inherent and potentially heroic wildness. The trouble with the pseudo-thunder is that it shares with "The Common Life" a flatness, an abstractness in the bad sense of being only two-dimensional. The most significant way in which the true artist is weak is that he is deliberately ignorant. Then he has "The Sense of the Sleight-of-Hand Man"—he is too slight of hand to try to piece the world together with his hands (as in "Parochial Theme," the first poem in *Parts of a World*). And so he surrenders himself to the sleight-of-hand that his eye accomplishes, or—as is implied in "Poem Written at Morning"—to the sleight-of-hand of the green-curled giant. In this state, in which the eye is actually much quicker than the hand, the minimum myth of the imagined pine and the imagined jay at the end of "Blue Guitar" expands into something bigger and deeper than myths as such: the jay swoops down from the pine, writing his name and his cry ("J") in the air, and this curve is then seen as part of a wheel—the spokes of which are the sun's rays. Then the pines become cornets announcing the mythless glory of the sun; and, in a sense, heaven is restored to an unconsciously believable existence as "a little island full of geese and stars."

The freshness of ignorance celebrated in "The Sleight-of-Hand Man" is essentially a visual one. In the next group of poems, from "The Candle a Saint" to "Yellow Afternoon," Stevens asserts that to let immediate experience pierce the abstract understanding is to confront life with all one's senses, not with eyesight alone. At the point of definition of the "I" who speaks with such exquisite gusto of the dish of peaches in Russia, the poet calls him "That animal, that Russian, that exile, for whom/The bells of the chapel pullulate sounds at/Heart." The tasting "I" is then the animal within anyone who finds himself the citizen of a modern state rather than the native of a place, a village; and he is an exile in his own land as long as he cannot actually taste and smell the peaches.

In "Arcades of Philadelphia the Past," the rich are as poor as the past they can only see. The apparently poor man, who cannot remember "strawberries once in the Apennines," is really rich because he lives in his five senses and in the this and the now. He can say of the strawberries, "They seem a little painted, now./The mountains are scratched and used, clear fakes." That is, he is a connoisseur of the real—the little unassuming man who is not duped by a polished but insipid nostalgia.

Characteristics of light alone, as in "Of Hartford in a Purple Light," may be feminine—that is, they may lose their masculine freshness unless fused with a quality of wetness. Or, as the figure changes in "Cuisine Bourgeoise," visual experience is all there is to the typically modern, scientific knowledge, which is a kind of memory, to the degree that it is like trying to eat a reflection of oneself. Like the purple light in the preceding poem, this "Cuisine Bourgeoise" is feminine.

There are no reflections, no perfectly matched data in "Forces, the Will, & the Weather." That is why the "peer yellow"—the perfectly equal yellow—sighs. Only in Moscow are there ideas like that of identical colors, such as science depends on. But here, with the white dog pulling the pink girl against her will, and with the pink and white dogwoods (dog would's or dog wills) resembling sheets, resembling nougats, all seems edible. Whereas in the preceding poem we are too late for the real meal, in this one we are in command of the whole feast of the sense. As the next poem, "On an Old Horn," puts it, the mere colors are "False as the mind, instead of the fragrance, warm/With sun." Or, in "Bouquet of Belle Scavoir," if the woman who embodies poetry (La Gaya Scienza, Die Fröhliche Wissenschaft: poetry) is only reflected in various colors, "The reflection of her here, and then there,/Is another shadow, another evasion,/Another denial." "It is she that he wants, to look at directly,/Someone before him to see and to know." And finally, "Variations on a Summer Day" confront us with the day in all its guises, until they all become transparent and she, the day, is like a naked woman.

If this group of poems suggest that mere eyesight is effeminate or sterile, "Yellow Afternoon" suggests that the unity of all the senses resembles "the fatal unity of war." In "Martial Cadenza" the poet can see the fatal unity of war brought to a head under the evening star, *la belle étoile,* which was "Patron and imager of the gold Don John"—of Hoon. Just as Hoon was "A light at the centre of many lights,/A man at the centre of men" ("Man and Bottle"), so also he descended "the loneliest air" and thus can be transposed into an instance of the fact that "The mind is the great poem of winter." As such, as a force at large in a vacuum, Hoon's mind-poem "lashes more fiercely than the wind,/As the mind, to find what will suffice, destroys/Romantic tenements of rose and ice." It is, therefore, as a violent mind of winter, without losing any of its radiance, that Hoon contains war as "A manner of thinking, a mode/Of destroying, as the mind destroys." Here one can see how "Blue Guitar" implicitly combined Hoon ("The amorist Adjective aflame . . .") with the mind of winter ("this picture of Picasso's, this 'hoard/Of destructions,' a picture of ourselves."); that is, in Part III of "Blue Guitar" the poet finds his identity as both a creator and a destroyer. Now the combination is becoming explicit. The fatal unity of war can be felt as the vital unity of Hoon.

"Of Modern Poetry" continues on the same theme of finding what will suffice, but it adds an emphasis on the *act* of the mind. In making this emphasis, it speaks also of "an invisible audience" which listens, not to the poem's action but to itself, "expressed/ In an emotion as of two people, as of two/Emotions becoming one." In "Arrival at the Waldorf" the invisible audience turns out to be the "wintry slime . . . of men in crowds" of "Farewell to Florida" who are transformed into "The world in a verse,/A generation sealed, men remoter than mountains,/Women invisible in music and motion and color." In *Ideas of Order* the poet was tempted to "expunge all people and be a pupil/Of the gorgeous wheel": to be "mountain-minded Hoon, . . . Who found all form and order in solitude,/For whom the shapes were never the figures of men." Now, if Hoon, by including the fatal unity of war can speak for and to an invisible audience, his emotion meeting theirs and the two emotions becoming one, then those oppressively present and intimate men in mobs become "remoter than mountains"; the women become "invisible in music and motion and color."

Under the pressure of war Stevens has accomplished what looked impossible in the depth of the Depression. As he said in "Sad Strains of a Gay Waltz,"

> Too many waltzes—The epic of disbelief
> Blares oftener and soon, will soon be constant.
> Some harmonious skeptic soon in a skeptical music
>
> Will unite these figures of men and their shapes
> Will glisten again with motion, the music
> Will be motion and full of shadows.

This expresses precisely the image of the women in "Arrival at the Waldorf." But, when Stevens wrote "Sad Strains of a Gay Waltz" early in 1935, he was full of the impossibility of such an image—as full as he was of the incongruity of trying to be Mozart in 1935.

But, in order for the men in mobs to glisten again with motion, they apparently must become remoter than mountains. They are then no better off than the "anti-master-man, floribund ascetic" in "Landscape with Boat." He says, "The thing I hum appears to be/The rhythm of this celestial pantomime," which has much the same import as the lines in "Arrival at the Waldorf": "you hum and the orchestra/Hums and you say 'The world is a verse,/A generation sealed. . . .'" What kind of truth does a generation sealed seek? At its best, this poem suggests, it rejects all immediate experience and supposes "A truth beyond all truths." Like the men at the beginning of "Blue Guitar," it wants "A tune beyond us as we are." It never supposes that "divine/ Things might not look divine, nor that if nothing/Was divine then all things were, the world itself,/And that if nothing was the truth, then all/Things were the truth, the world itself was the truth." Such people haven't the imagination to become ignorant men, as in "The Sense of the Sleight-of-Hand Man": they never make the bare, sensuous contact between the empty self in empty space; they think too much. The rational will that was so carefully rejected in the first poems of *Parts of a World* reappears here as an exaggerated form of vulgarity.

The next poem, "On the Adequacy of Landscape," makes the contrast complete: the people in the air are frightened by "the bright, discursive wings" of the little owl of Minerva—thought— and so are unable "in their empty hearts to feel/The blood-red redness of the sun."

> So that he that suffers most desires
> The red bird most and the strongest sky—
> Not the people in the air that hear
> The little owl fly.

"Les Plus Belles Pages," according to the implications of Stevens' own exegesis of it (*OP*, 293), adds that the man who accepts the world—rather than looking beyond ("He spoke,/Kept speaking, of God. I changed the word to man.")—must be a man in whom thought and emotion interact, rather than one who is all one or the other. This idea is only implicit in "Les Plus Belles Pages," but it receives its classical statement in "Notes Toward a Supreme Fiction" where it is made clear from the start that "One must become an ignorant man again," with the emphasis on the "again." It takes thought to ignore thought. Then thought, which in much of Stevens' poetry is a tyrannous master, becomes, as in "Poem with Rhythms," "the powerful mirror of my wish and will": that is, a powerful but obedient servant. In "Woman Looking at a Vase of Flowers" the little owl of Minerva serves the woman's wish and will by showing her the composition of particulars into which "the crude/And jealous grandeurs of sun and sky/Scattered themselves."

And yet "It can never be satisfied, the mind, never." In "The Well Dressed Man with a Beard," the same power of composition—thought—would try to compose experience by rejecting everything rather than by bringing everything into harmony. Then, if only one thing were left after such a rejection—like the little bristles on the face of a man who dressed himself well enough in the morning but forgot to shave—the same power would be dissatisfied. "Woman Looking at a Vase of Flowers" and "The Well Dressed Man with a Beard" are in combination a repetition of "The Poems of Our Climate," which asserts near the end "There would still remain the never-resting mind."

"Never" is perhaps an exaggeration; at least the next poem, "Of Bright & Blue Birds & the Gala Sun," proclaims that there are moments when "we are joyously ourselves and we think/ Without the labor of thought, in that element,/And we feel, in a way apart, for a moment, as if/There was a bright *scienza* outside of ourselves." (The reader recalls the woman, Belle Scavoir; here *la gaya scienza* is the poetic *mundo*; together they form the green, flowing *mundo* which the poet addresses as "fat girl" at the end of "Notes.")

At this point, where the relations between thought and feeling seem to be nearing a definition, Stevens seems to abandon the effort. Or, rather, he accepts the seesaw motion between sun and moon that he had resigned himself to in "Comedian." In "Mrs. Alfred Uruguay," for instance, this lady is a more intense version of the floribund ascetic in "Landscape with Boat": "Her no and no made yes impossible." The other alternative is not some fusion of her moonlight "no" with the sunlight "yes," but "a rider intent on the sun": the figure of the youth as virile poet as noble rider. So the hero makes his first appearance. But it is a somewhat unbalanced appearance: it violently counterbalances the excess of negative determination on the part of Mrs. Alfred Uruguay and her donkey.

In "Asides on the Oboe" the hero appears more explicitly, and a series of poems begins that is generally devoted to the hero. Explicitly the hero is

> The impossible possible philosophers' man,
> The man who has had the time to think enough,
> The central man, the human globe, responsive
> As a mirror with a voice, the man of glass,
> Who in a million diamonds sums us up.

"Impossible possible" is peculiarly precise. The way in which Stevens resolves the conflict between thought and feeling is already implicit in the original complementary opposition between nothingness and life. Wintry nothingness has a power of rejection that thought never dreamed of, and yet winter devises summer in its breast. Similarly in "Asides on the Oboe," "The glass man, cold and numbered, dewily cries,/'Thou art not August unless I make thee so.'" Or, even more to the point,

since war is now a far more threatening thing than nothingness
ever showed itself to be in *Harmonium,*

> One year, death and war prevented the jasmine scent
> And the jasmine islands were bloody martyrdoms.
> How was it then with the central man? Did we
> Find peace? We found the sum of men. We found,
> If we found the central evil, the central good.
> We buried the fallen without jasmine crowns.
> There was nothing he did not suffer, no; nor we.

As in "Man with Bottle," the hero in "Asides on the Oboe" is
a Hoon-like figure who by including in his self the experience of
war, the central evil, also includes the central good, creating
that good out of that evil, like the figure of the crow in "No
Possum, No Sop, No Taters" ("Bright is the malice in his eye").
Hence the hero must become an ignorant man—a man of pure
feeling—again and again, just as, by the same compulsion, he
must become pure thought again and again. He must submit to
his rational will, and then he must make that will his absolute
servant.

"Extracts from Addresses to the Academy of Fine Ideas," like
"Asides on the Oboe," reconciles good and evil in the life-and-
death of the soldier hero. The "men in helmets" in the last two
lines of the poem are heroic because they know in their hearts
that they are going to defeat: like Achilles, they live at the top
of their bent because they know they are going to die.

"Montrachet-le-Jardin" presents a more unpretentious image
of the hero:

> Consider how the speechless, invisible gods
> Ruled us before, from over Asia, by
> Our merest apprehension of their will.
>
> There must be mercy in Asia and divine
> Shadows of scholars bent upon their books,
> Divine orations from lean sacristans
>
> Of the good, speaking of good in the voice of men.
> All men can speak of it in the voice of gods.
> But to speak simply of good is like to love,
>
> To equate the root-man and the super-man,
> The root-man swarming, tortured by his mass,
> The super-man friseured, possessing and possessed.

After bringing the gods down to heroic human proportions, Stevens speaks of the continuing human origins of heroism: the root-man. But, in doing so, he reverses the values that he expressed in "Owl's Clover," where there was no hope, either in the subman or in the sprawling portent that grew out of him. Here the root-man is "swarming, tortured by his mass," but the super-man is "friseured, possessing and possessed." "Friseured" may remind the reader of Crispin and of the woman in "Le Monocle," to mention only two of the curly-haired personages in Stevens' theatrical company. But the nearest analogue is the giant in "Poem Written at Morning": "Green were the curls on that head." The giant or the hero is now more easily and constantly imagined. As in "Mrs. Alfred Uruguay," Stevens is approaching the affirmative mood of "Notes," in which the hero can appear as an infant or as a soldier in old clothes, home on leave, and have for mother and inamorata the fat girl. In other words, he can be completely ordinary and still remain heroic.

Or so Stevens says. What the hero is in fact doing toward the end of "Montrachet-le-Jardin"—beholding "the grace/And free requiting of responsive fact,/To project the naked man in a state of fact,/As acutest virtue and ascetic trove"—comes to an end abruptly: "I affirm and then at midnight the great cat/Leaps quickly from the fireside and is gone." And while the great cat of liquid perceptions is away, the macabre mice come back to play. "The News and the Weather" is satire of the *Ideas of Order* sort, coupled with a vaguely optimistic echo of "Like Decorations in a Nigger Cemetery." "Metamorphosis" reverses the usual "Winter devising summer in its breast," adroitly stopping the optimistic bent of the previous poem. The contrary theses of death and life, and implicitly of death and life *versus* the vulgar, are balanced, just as fruition and war are balanced in "Contrary Theses (I)."

Fruition and war form, of course, the most fecund conflict for Stevens; and the six following poems are in general optimistic. "Phosphor Reading by his Own Light" repeats the gist of "The Candle a Saint": "Green is the night." "The Search for Sound Free from Motion" at least holds out the hope that the world can embody, by speaking the poet's language, a motionless sound—can balance "The syllable of a syllable." That would seem to be possible for

> The companion in nothingness,
> Loud, general, large, fat, soft
> And wild and free, the secondary man

who so completely *is* the world that "There are no rocks/And stones, only this imager." "Contrary Theses (II)" only momentarily brakes the happy mood by balancing the vulgar against life and death. Its last sentence may be a resolution ("The flies/ And the bees still sought the chrysanthemums' odor") for the next poem, "The Hand as a Being," which goes farther than any other poem by Stevens to create a figure in which the rational will, which Stevens represents by hands (in "Parochial Theme" and in "Poem with Rhythms"), is made synonymous with desire. The excessive consciousness of "our man" in the poem is probably intended as a weeping-burgher kind of vulgarity; and the hand-gesture of "the naked, nameless dame" is, at least in one obvious aspect, a quite ordinary sort of vulgarity. And yet she accomplishes a true sleight-of-hand; it expresses and elicits a reciprocity of desires that seize and compose and simplify "our man," the way "The wind had seized the tree

> and ha, and ha,
> It held the shivering, the shaken limbs,
> Then bathed its body in the leaping lake.

"Oak Leaves Are Hands" seems to be an effort to carry this image still farther but with no success.

"Examination of the Hero in a Time of War" virtually sums up Stevens' thematic development to date. In parts I-IV the old romance of God's bright arms saving man is projected and rejected, the rejection made final by the Chopin parody in IV. As I pointed out in discussing *Harmonium*, Stevens found the vulgar Christian idea of the afterlife to be the most obnoxious obstruction between life and death. In parts V-XI, developing the idea that the common man must be the common hero, the image of him as a person is rejected; this rejection is made final by the parody in XI, the parade of the dry description. The attitude expressed in XI may have dictated the rejection of "Owl's Clover" from the "Collected Poems"; its sprawling portent was too much described and not enough rendered. The frustrated effort to make of the common man something other than the oppressively vulgar thing that he was during the Depression is the theme of *Ideas of Order*. Parts XII-XVI expound the idea of the hero as a feeling of heroism that men can all experience. This idea is developed to the point where the feeling itself ("man-sun being hero") can reject an excessive abstraction of itself, and thereby return and remain the familiar man, whose works and pastimes are these: "he studies the paper/On the wall, the lemons on the table."

The development of feelings of heroism and an arrival at a new feeling of wholeness, harmony, and radiance are the burden of "Blue Guitar" and *Parts of a World*; and this new feeling continued to pervade Stevens' poetry almost until the end of his life. Only in his last poems, when, presumably, he was face to face with the vulgarity that the war did not *permanently* transfigure, did he, as in "The Plain Sense of Things," admit that the glow was gone and that all that was left was the vulgar plainly seen. But Stevens insists that it is something to have acted on the necessity to see this vulgarity, and it may be that in the long run his action on that necessity will remain his noblest action.

CHAPTER 3

Transport to Summer

IN HIS AUTOBIOGRAPHY Yeats says, "How could I judge any scheme of education, or of social reform, when I could not measure what the different classes and occupations contributed to that invisible commerce of reverie and sleep: and what is luxury and what necessity when a fragment of gold braid, or a flower in the wallpaper may be an originating impulse to revolution or to philosophy?"[1] Such reflections made Yeats feel "not only solitary but helpless" because he was trying to help lead the Irish nationalist movement. Similar reflections, as the reader has just noticed, had the opposite effect on Stevens; his man-sun-hero necessarily, deliberately, and happily "studies the paper on the wall." And Stevens is reassured, not only because he was twice Yeats's age, at the time, and not only because he was not and never had been involved in political action, but chiefly because solitude and helplessness and ordinariness were his confirmed conditions, the weaknesses in which he found his greatest powers.

Nowhere does Stevens express this assurance more convincingly than in "Notes," which was published at the beginning of the period in which the poems in *Transport to Summer* were published. He placed "Notes" at the end of that volume, apparently to indicate that the poems collected there are better read as preparations for the reading of his masterpiece, "Notes," rather than as afterthoughts; and I believe it can be demonstrated that he was right.

The poems in *Transport* are printed in what is roughly the order of publication. The poems newly published with the book seem to be inserted at various points to mark the ends of sequences, each of which has a particular emphasis or concern.

These marker poems divide *Transport* into five parts: the first states the general argument of the book ("there is here"); the second shows how that argument works in the public or social world; the third, in the private or personal world; the fourth, in the world of language *per se*; and the fifth, "Notes," is the myth complete.

"God Is Good. It Is a Beautiful Night" is the first of a series of poems, ending with "Crude Foyer," that deal with certain implications of Stevens' adagium, "Life is an affair of people not of places. But for me life is an affair of places and that is the trouble." One of these implications is made more explicit than anywhere else in the last line of "Crude Foyer": "content/At last, there, when it turns out to be here." The place, the landscape, that Stevens is always seeking to live in, must finally be a present one, both in time and space, both interior and exterior. And from this implication flows another: that he need not move in order to find his paradisal place. As we have seen, this second implication was emphasized at the end of *Parts of a World*, in "Examinations of the Hero in a Time of War," XV: "These are the works and pastimes/Of the highest self: he studies the paper/On the wall, the lemons on the Table."

The personae of the first group of poems in *Transport to Summer* are not only more like places and times than people, but they are also carefully *present* place-time-personae and steadfastly *immobile*. In "God Is Good. It Is a Beautiful Night" the moon at the end of summer is a bird that flies, but the poet is a head on the ground. An empty shoe somewhere nearby indicates that walking is out of the question. Furthermore, the poet bids the moon-bird "Look round at the head and zither/On the ground" before it flies, and the poet's song is said to be "The song of the great *space*" (my italics) of the moon-bird's age. The poem renders the stasis after the violent maximum of summer, a stasis in which disembodiment is made to show its prettiest and at the same time its grimmest *fin de siècle* face. The title is heavily ironical; if there must be a god in this non-house, then god is bad. It is a horrible night. And yet it is a "fresh night." What makes it horrible rather than merely grim is that it is freshly stabbed to death by the disembodied poet's song.

The grimness of the place-personae of "God Is Good" relaxes into the neglect, the leisure, and the convalescence of the place-time-personae of "Certain Phenomena of Sound." Now a spider spins in the empty shoe; but the once-passionate man, old John Rocket, only dozes on his pillow. Life is suspended, not ended. It is apparently late summer, a natural pause in the turning of time. The silence of the telephone, the withering of the geranium, the absence of the cat, the sound of the locusts, the departure of someone "for a ride in a balloon"—all these compose a *safe* nothingness.

It is a nothingness in which one can gladly hear and believe Redwood Roamer's tall tale, and believe it so completely, so repletely with fruit and wine and music, that the narrative is "A sound producing the things that are spoken." Or, for another example, this natural phenomenon of leisure is like the circumstance of being a patient in a hospital. It is a blank, like a parasol opened wide against the sun, in which a name spoken or written —Old John Rocket, Redwood Roamer, Eulalia, Semiramide—creates the person named.

The situation in "Certain Phenomena" is directly opposite to that in "God Is Good." "God Is Good" represents the end of the imagination; "Certain Phenomena" represents its beginning. In "The Motive for Metaphor" the atmosphere of hospitality and hospitalization in parts II and III of "Certain Phenomena" is generalized into all times when one desires "the exhilirations of changes." The end of such changes is "The weight of primary noon"; at that point in time (and space) the poet is beheaded and the imagination stops, as in "God Is Good." A moment afterward, the spider spins in his empty shoe, and the changes begin again, as in "Certain Phenomena."

In "The Motive for Metaphor" "the wind moves like a cripple among the leaves," continuing the tendency toward immobility in this first group of poems. "Gigantomachia" begins, "They could not carry much, as soldiers," and it all but ends with "Each man himself became a giant,/Tipped out with largeness, bearing the heavy/And the high,/Receiving out of others,/As from an inhuman elevation/And origin, an inhuman person." The suggestion is that each soldier becomes a mountain. The reader is on his way to the majestic calm of "Chocorua to its Neighbor."

The last line of "Gigantomachia" is, "For soldiers, the new moon stretches twenty feet." In the gathering strength of motive for metaphor, under conditions of increasing immobility, even the moon, which was a rather sinister brown bird in "God Is Good," is becoming auspicious.

In "Dutch Graves in Bucks County" the soldiers of World War II are rising to a new, deliberately suicidal height of heroism, while the buried religious Dutch soldiers inaudibly cheer them on. The religious Dutch fought for "the glory of heaven in the wilderness," and this makes them sympathetic with "a new glory of new men," a glory of men who kill their past selves every day. Therefore the religious Dutch are more recognizable as "semblables" than ancient heroes who lived and fought and died as lustily as the sun rises and sets, and are "lost/In an ignorance of sleep with nothing won." It was part of that ignorance to will their defeats to their descendants, and so to perpetuate their tragedy. Both the religious Dutch and the modern soldiers avoid this tragedy by *knowingly* going to their death; they know before they go that their lives and their deaths are absolutely new each day and each night. The central import of the poem is the paradox that there is more continuity between these deliberately discontinuous generations than there was in the ancient world, where the generations were deliberately continuous.

The final metaphor is that of a spiral: a generation does not move in a line that is continued in the next generation. It spirals inward toward the center of its consciousness, toward a point of view from which it can see the whole of its life and its death and at which it is free to choose that whole in all its actuality. An inheritance from the preceding generation blinds one to the discreteness of each generation and so prevents one from seeking the center and making the choice. The last two lines in the poem—"Time was not wasted in your subtle temples./No: nor divergence made too steep to follow down"—suggest that generations that are self-consciously discrete are like cones that coincide at the large end but come to their points in different places, the Dutch in heaven, the present-day soldiers on earth. Then generations that deceive themselves with the belief that they are continuous are like a circle that repeats itself. The perpetually perfect repetition is a waste of time because the generations, not seeing any difference between each other, never know themselves or each other, and so cannot sympathize with each other or learn from each other. The image of eccentric circles, circles that do not repeat one another exactly, became increasingly prominent in the later poetry.

In "No Possum, No Sop, No Taters," Stevens turns from a summer-maximum image to a winter-minimum. This shift is a characteristic expression of his insatiable desire to see the whole cycle of the seasons in one comprehensive image, or to see his whole world of birth, copulation, and death in one glance. But what is most interesting in this group of poems is what happens to the images of immobility and presence. The combination of modern soldiers in the sky and Dutch religious soldiers under the ground tends toward a cosmic image. In "No Possum," which may be a pun on the Latin verb, "I am not able," contracts that almost cosmic image in "Dutch Graves" into one of *un*buried dead, or personae so dismembered and so stuck in the ice that they might as well be dead, and one of a balancing transcendence that is also carefully limited. Like the crow, one also rises only as high as a tree; and that tree must be as rooted in the ice as the cornstalks are.

Otherwise, the import of "No Possum" is similar to that of "Dutch Graves":

> It is here, in this bad, that we reach
> The last purity of the knowledge of good.
>
> The crow looks rusty as he rises up.
> Bright is the malice in his eye . . .

The tiny but intense spark of life shown by an angel of death indicates that death, or an impotence like it, the worst evil known to Stevens' body-like spirit, is as good as life—if one understands "good" to mean a modern self-conscious version of the ancient heroic virtues. Regarded in this way, death is what Stevens was to call a year later, in "Esthetique du Mal," "the happiest enemy." If one dies knowingly in combat with such a force, one dies nobly, happily, innocently, and well.

Just as Stevens must turn from the summer maximum to the winter minimum, as in following "Dutch Graves" with "No Possum," so he must turn from the grimly earnest to the lightly earnest and follow "No Possum" with "So-and-So Reclining on Her Couch." The figure, the painter's model as she appears in the painting, is not dismembered as in "God Is Good" and "No Possum"; or dozing or convalescing, as in "Certain Phenomena"; or almost mountainous, as in "Gigantomachia"; or buried or moving inward, as in "Dutch Graves." She is new born, at age twenty-one, and reclining motionless. She has three aspects: a natural one, herself as a model, a living person; an artificial one, the crowned figure the painter puts on the canvas; and the flux back and forth between the two, "Between the thing as idea and/The idea as thing." She is espoused by a man whose name means Double-Daddy, because she is loved and made pregnant (the flux) both as a real woman and as an imagined woman. But her offspring ("and thanks") is "the world/As anything but sculpture." That is, the result of confronting and analyzing the contention between reality and imagination in the appearance of anything is a renewed confidence in appearance as itself sufficient: "One walks easily the unpainted shore." One should notice as well, though, that the poet says goodbye to Mrs. Pappadopoulos and thanks, rather abruptly. She is a throwaway persona, a form of dehumanization more complete than any of the others in this group of poems.

If Mrs. Pappadopoulos represents the extreme limit of dehumanization, Chocorua's shadow, the persona described and celebrated in "Chocorua to its Neighbor," represents the beginning of a movement in the opposite direction: a place and a time that can just barely be seen as human. What is most interesting about this minimal humanity is that it is also, to Stevens, "more than human." The shadow of Chocorua is so large that it is "part/Of sky, of sea, large earth, large air" and so "To think of him destroyed the body's form." To be so all-inclusive is to be both formless and god-like.

But Stevens avoids vulgar pantheism by concentrating on the actual appearance of the shadow, by putting himself in the place of the mountain, and by speaking out of his own sense of freedom, in the presence of the shadow, to perceive everything at once.

> He [the shadow] breathed in crystal-pointed change the whole
> Experience of night, as if he breathed
> A consciousness from solitude, inhaled
> A freedom out of silver-shaping size,
> Against the whole experience of day.

The last line of this passage points to the other remarkable thing about the shadow as a barely human, superhuman persona: it is *night's* omniconsciousness, brought down to a barely definable shape. Chocorua does most of the talking, as the title indicates, and as a mountain it speaks from a certain height of human awareness. But it speaks of its shadow, a form of the night that never leaves it and which, as a form of the night, has depths that are fatal and a height that is starry. The acceptance of the dark side of human nature expressed in this poem is unusual for Stevens; a frightened and therefore cautious stance is more typical, as in "Thirteen Ways of Looking at a Blackbird" and "No Possum, No Sop, No Taters." But along with the confidence that Stevens could see through and absorb the vulgar, which he gained in writing "Blue Guitar," he became more and more able to say, as in that poem,

> Throw away the lights, the definitions,
> And say of what you see in the dark
> That it is this or that it is that,
> But do not use the rotted names.

That is, he came to see the unconscious more and more as Jung's fountain rather than as Freud's cellar-hole; and in "A Word with José Rodriguez-Feo," a poem published less than a year after "Chocorua," he can say almost smugly, "Night is the nature of man's interior world."

Or, closer at hand, "Poesie Abrutie" treats a scene that seems to be self-consciously only a month later than that in "No Possum," with a mixture of relief and regret. Stevens' motive for metaphor was strongest in transitional states, like a mountain's shadow which is part of night but strongest when night departs or like the smallest signs of the end of winter in February. But he yearned for the power to respond imaginatively to the full depth (as in "No Possum") and to the full height (as in "Credences of Summer"), and he moved *away from* those challenges with a note of self-disgust, as in "Poesie Abrutie." He was happiest when he was moving *toward* the height or the depth: hence the titles *Transport to Summer* and *Auroras of Autumn*, the latter being, whether intended or not, an extended prelude to "The Rock," his most ambitious attempt at a metaphor for all seasons included in one. That he was finally satisfied with an all-inclusive image of the cold, the dark, the empty, and the rock-like is a measure of his final maturity, both as a poet and as a man.

In "The Lack of Repose" the movement toward the maximum is described as putting "a momentary end/To the complication" in a book that one has not yet written, and which therefore cannot be read with easy confidence by one's grandson. Thus one avoids both a false sense of the end in his own movement toward the center of his generation and a false sense of continuity with following generations.

In "Somnambulisma" the true sense of discontinuity, explicit in "Dutch Graves" and implicit in "The Lack of Repose," is rendered by a metaphor of the ocean rolling "on an old shore" like a bird "That thinks of settling, yet never settles, on a nest." The human ocean which, according to this metaphor, both generates and washes away all its generations would be "a geography of the dead," would lack "a pervasive being," if it were not imagined as a bird. Only the imagination can give conscious life to the endless somnambulism.

"Crude Foyer" is a marker poem, one newly published with the book *Transport to Summer*; and it was apparently inserted, anachronistically, to mark the end of a group of related poems. Part of the argument of "Crude Foyer" comes as something of a jolt: "that/We are ignorant men incapable/Of the least, minor, vital metaphor." This statement comes right after the conclusion of "Somnambulisma," in which the imagination "Poured forth the fine fins, the gawky beaks, the personalia" that give life to the world. What justifies this exaggeration in the argument of "Crude Foyer" is its attempt to push the reasoning implicit in all the poems we have just been considering to an explicit statement: the place, the landscape, that Stevens is always seeking to live in must finally be a present one, both in time and in space, both interior and exterior. In other words, Stevens is moving toward his own version of "A rose is a rose is a rose" or, in words from "So-and-So," toward an "unpainted shore."

The next group of poems, from "Repetitions of a Young Captain" to "Sketch of the Ultimate Politician," tends to look on the here and now as significantly social or political. The reader may recall in "The Glass of Water" that "the centre of our lives, this time, this day,/It is a state, this spring among the politicians/

Playing cards." But the tone of the political and social poems in *Transport to Summer*, like those in *Ideas of Order*, is angry, satirical, but not heavily so; Stevens was apparently always annoyed by the pressure of society and by the very idea of publicity.

The group begins with "Repetitions of a Young Captain," which follows from the "unpainted shore" motif in an almost Stein-like manner: "It was something overseas/That I remembered, something that I remembered/Overseas, that stood in an external world." The slight variation in the two statements leaves the *place* of the thing remembered ambiguous: is it something that the captain saw overseas and then remembered when he returned to the United States, or is it something in the United States that he remembered when he was overseas? The ambiguity is intentional, and is of the nature of the there-is-here paradox at the end of "Crude Foyer." As the captain says, "Constantly,/At the railway station, a soldier steps away,/Sees a familiar building drenched in cloud/And goes to an external world, having/Nothing of place."

The captain becomes first "the giant of sense," the tempestuous present force of reality, ruining the past; and then the captain becomes himself again—himself as an accumulation of his past. The whole of his experience includes both the giant present and the "powdered personals," the theatrical past; and he seeks a point between the two, as did the soldiers in "Dutch Graves." The past and the present push themselves away from this midpoint: the past says, "Secrete me from reality," pushing herself back from the present into the unconscious. The present says "That reality secrete itself," pushing himself forward into the unknowable. The captain (or the poet) seeks his point between the two, the center of consciousness, from which he can say both "It was something overseas that I remembered" and "It was something I remembered overseas." Ambiguity becomes paradox; mutually exclusive alternatives have become absorbed and harmonized in a concrete universal: "Secrete us in reality." In other words, put us, with all our past selves, so completely into the present moment that we are no longer weakened by the unreality of those past selves and have instead all the strength of the present moment. But, given that present strength, we no longer need the gigantic anger which our effete past at first inspired. So the giantness, too, falls down and comes to nothing. Then we are without personality of any kind, gigantic or ghostly. We have "a civil nakedness," an anonymity that is like a secret being. Hence, "Secrete us in reality."

I believe "Repetitions" is a social or political poem because it takes its departure and its imagery from the condition of war, and specifically World War II, as a climactic and present instance of the destruction of one kind of imagination and the beginning of another. And the poem expresses the impatience and anger characteristic of Stevens' more topical poems.

In "The Creations of Sound," X sounds like MacLeish, a poet who is "too exactly himself" and who does not "make the visible a little hard/To see." He is apparently both too public, or even too political, and too personal; he does not try to secrete himself in reality. "Holiday in Reality" is about painters who, like X, in "The Creations of Sound," haven't the internal "unreal" sense of their own personal colors. These painters are *not* on holiday in reality. They are aware that there is no common man or common speech, and yet their paintings are not private.

"Esthetique du Mal" is Stevens' longest treatment of the problem of evil. It fits into this series of "public" poems because of its curious political emphasis in the next to the last part of it. Its argument runs roughly as follows:

I: Vesuvius and the past feel no pain when they cause or suffer destruction.

II: The moon is indifferent to men, and by rejecting men, it saves them.

III: The trouble is with an over-human god, who pities men too much and so encourages them to pity themselves.

IV: The pity of Christ is sentimental—pity for everyone, rather than for the one that one loves most. Whoever comes to fight Satan must fight an unsentimental, egotistical idealist.

V: The unity of affection for real people obviates the pursuit of golden forms.

VI: The search for golden forms (Platonism) is ridiculous and futile.

VII: For instance, real redness is in death and in life (a perfect form exists here and now in life).

VIII: Even the death of Satan, tragic as it was for the imagination, is only the end of one image for evil, and therefore the beginning of another.

IX: Likewise, the moon's loss of its imaginary meanings encourages a new fecundity, a new plenitude, in the midst of the destitution and the indifference that the moon's new meaninglessness has left behind.

X: Even the nostalgic image of "Mother," if it is of the one person (as in Part V) who is "reality" itself, can prove a man "against the touch of inpersonal pain," disentangle him from "sleek ensolacings," because in unity with her ("reality") he can find his *innocence*, both in his life and in his death.

XI: Efforts to sweeten the deaths of all kinds of people fail to satisfy the man who has found the innocence he has in his mother. Then the hungriness that is left, not having these sweets to glut it, is itself a thing to eat, a satisfaction.

XII: The hungriness that is left is "a third world without knowledge,/In which no one peers, in which the will makes no/ Demands." That is, it is neither peopled nor unpeopled, neither social nor purely personal. In this third world of absolute ignorance, privacy, and poverty, the poet can accept everything, including pain. But, lacking his own will and lacking other people, he cannot love: there is no joy in this world.

XIII: In X, it was his mother that restored to him his innocence, disentangled him from the sleek ensolacings of XI, and left him with the third world of satisfying hungriness in XII. His example of what that third world lacks in the way of someone to love is "what woman,/However known, at the centre of the heart?" XIII begins, "It may be that one life is a punishment for another, as the son's life for the father's." The suggestion is that the woman missing from the third world is the mother: the actual *personal* mother who is seen as "reality." This section begins by suggesting a personal, genealogical source for evil, and then proceeds to reject that possibility, with the statement, "But that concerns the secondary characters./It is a fragmentary tragedy/Within the universal whole." Personal characters are secondary; archetypal ones, primary. "The unalterable necessity of being this unalterable animal" is a primary, archetypal tragedy. In it, "the force of nature in action," "the happiest enemy," "discloses himself." A man in the third world may establish this tragedy in a vision of "the fire-feinting sea" (cf. "Fire Monsters in the Milky Brain")—the destructive fire in the mother-sea, the destructive-creative sea, "a reality of the longest meditation." That tragedy man can only endure "with the politest help-lessness."

XIV: The singularity and the necessity of the tragedy of each generation ("the son/And the father alike and equally are spent") makes Stevens think of the Russian revolution, which expressed a sentimental love for all people, rejecting the senti-mentality of Christ's love for all people and believing that a new good would arise out of the ruins of a rejected past. The loves, rejections, and beliefs of a revolution constitute the emotion of politics pursued in a certain single-minded way. Stevens' "politics of emotion" is similarly single-minded; the "adventure to be en-dured with the *politest* [my italics] helplessness" is "the unalter-able necessity/of being this unalterable animal." The difference between Konstantinov and Stevens is that Konstantinov "would have all the people/Live, work, suffer, and die in that idea [his single-minded idea of revolution]/In a world of ideas," whereas Stevens insists that everyone in fact *does* live, work, suffer, and die almost blindly in a self or a world which he can fully see only when he *does not* live, work, suffer, or die, and only when he sees it in the master-metaphor of destruction-creation, the ocean. Then he knows that his tragedy is only one among many, one small part of the whole; and he is not deceived and martyred by a logic of one idea which he sees reflected as by a lake, by the whole world. ("The lake at Geneva" suggests Calvin and the early poem, "The Doctor of Geneva.") Konstantinov would not even be aware of the lake: he would not be aware that it was only one lake, not the whole world. He is a lunatic because he is not aware that his lake is like the moon, an old has-been re-flector that now reflects nothing real (as in parts II and IX). The influence of the lake, like the old influence of the moon, is subconscious, even though its lucidity encourages logic. Thus it makes him a "logical lunatic," and it makes his "extreme of logic" "illogical."

XV: Such an illogical logic, such a logical lunacy is "non-physical"; and in the non-physical paradise that it projects, non-physical people like Konstantinov may experience their mi-nor fragmentary part of the whole major world or self that the physical people feel. "The greatest poverty is not to live/In a physical world," because

> . . . out of what one sees and hears and out
> Of what one feels, who could have thought to make
> So many selves, so many sensuous worlds,
> As if the air, the mid-day air, was swarming
> With the metaphysical changes that occur,
> Merely in living as and where we live.

Not only "The total past felt nothing when destroyed" (the last line of Part I), but each physical self felt nothing when it was destroyed a fraction of a second ago, and now, and now, and now. The self and its world, taken as completely physical, suffer death and rebirth every moment; and they create out of their new sights and sounds a multitude of selves and worlds that makes the heavenly hosts of the old Christian imagination, and of the more recent revolutionary imagination, look minor by comparison.[2]

The poems immediately following "Esthetique du Mal" elaborate or refine its more salient ideas. In "The Bed of Old John Zeller," Old John Zeller, Stevens' mother's father, was one of the non-physical people, but one whom Stevens could not shrug off as a logical lunatic as easily as he could Konstantinov. "In the old peak of might," seeing things from a godly point of view, even old John Zeller's ghostly sequences have an enviable orderliness. Placed where it is this poem might be taken as suggesting that Stevens was not happy about the rather anfractuous sequence of parts in "Esthetique du Mal." But, at the same time, he is proud that he can at least try to do the difficult thing that he attempts in "Esthetique du Mal," and in most of his poems: "to evade/That habit of wishing and to accept the structure/Of things as the structure of ideas."

Stevens was unwilling to attack his grandfather's *religious attitude*, but he was as eager as ever, in "Less and Less Human, O Savage Spirit," to demolish his grandfather's *god* and to substitute for it the unhearing, unseeing, unspeaking god of nothingness that he, Stevens, could believe in. At the end of "Esthetique du Mal," however, he emphasizes the infinite possibilities implicit in his own religious attitude: "any stick of the mass/Of which we are too distantly a part." But in "Less and Less Human" the tone is one of irritation, rather than wonder; it is a matter of indifference to him which stick is taken as an object of worship since all are equally god-like.

In "Wild Ducks, People and Distances," man is too distantly a part of and apart from the incommunicable mass because the lives of people separate him from the weather, which, if he were like *wild* ducks, would call him to migrate season by season. The implication is that man is like tame ducks who do not respond to seasonal changes in the weather and so are not alive. And yet "the life of the world depends on that he [anyone capable of it] is/Alive."

After calling "the unalterable necessity/Of being this unalterable animal" "the major tragedy" and "the happiest enemy" in Part XIII of "Esthetique du Mal," Stevens speculates that

> . . . it may be
> That in his Mediterranean cloister a man,
> Reclining, eased of desire, establishes
> The visible, a zone of blue and orange
> Versicolorings, establishes a time
> To watch the fire-feinting sea and calls it good,
> The ultimate good, . . .

"The Pure Good of Theory" begins by calling *time* "the hooded enemy"; and by his metaphors for time—a horse in the heart, a horse at night, a late walker, and breathing—the poet suggests that time is the aspect of physical necessity which is most immediately apprehensible. The cloistered and reclining man in Part XIII of "Esthetique du Mal" (perhaps Santayana) establishes an identity between "the visible" and "a time to watch," the latter being a time when one is "eased of desire," a time when one is not troubled by the horse in his heart or by his breathing. But one cannot arrive at such an untroubled, and therefore felicitous time, except through the troubling experience of palpable time. Thus time contains *All the Preludes to Felicity.*

But the "large-sculptured, platonic person" proposed in Part I of "The Pure Good of Theory" and then described in Part II is a ridiculous figure because he is completely non-physical. The figure in "Esthetique du Mal" (XIII) is not ridiculous because, if he is a Platonist, he is a materialistic one, like Santayana, who finds the ultimate good in the *visible*, the physical, not in "a soul

in the world." The platonic person only *dreams* of Brazil's av-
oirdupois; and the sense of happiness that Brazil gives him makes
him sick, more than it nourishes him, because it makes him won-
der if a paradise outside of time is only a sense and "beyond
intelligence." The trouble is that Brazil is only a "holiday" hotel,
flies only "the flag" of the nude; it is only a superficial, token
escape from the past, which the platonic person preserves within
him, as a Jew who has lived all his life in a European ghetto
might.

Part III, "*Fire Monsters in the Milky Brain*," contrasts Stevens'
own serious "knowledge of/Belief, that what it believes in is not
true," with the escapist romantic platonism ridiculed in Part II.
His rejection of old myths of transcendence is so thoroughgoing
that he can recognize that the *absence* of those myths is a new
myth, "the whole world as metaphor," and "Is still to stick to the
contents of the mind/And the desire to believe in a metaphor."
This is an escapism that recognizes itself as both inevitable and
impossible.

Part IV, "*Dry Birds are Fluttering in Blue Leaves*," explains
and celebrates this paradox; and it begins with the essence of
the matter: "It is never the thing but the version of the thing"
(that we believe in, and the version is not true because it is not
the thing itself). Then, out of this simple explanation come some
of the poet's gaudiest and homeliest metaphors, examples of
versions of the thing that both destroy the thing and replace it
with something happier or more arresting, and a final image of
fire and light that conveys both Heraclitus' stress on flux and
Plato's on commanding essences. But none of these metaphors
within the poem is as convincing or arresting as that of the title.
"Birds are fluttering in leaves" clearly attempts to name the
thing itself, but "Dry Birds are Fluttering in Blue Leaves" is so
true and yet so strange that the adjectives "dry" and "blue" seem
to have transformed the whole world. What makes this poem
part of the group of social and political poems is the satire on
the platonic person. The metaphors for his escapism—Brazil, the
holiday hotel, the flag of the nude, a Jew from Europe—are
easily reversible: both the malady and its symptoms are com-
mon, and they continue to interfere with the vision of even the
most imaginative men.

One such imaginative man is the poet, José Rodriguez-Feo,

whom Stevens honors with a word of fatherly reassurance, "A Word with José Rodriguez-Feo."

> As one of the secretaries of the moon,
> The queen of ignorance, you have deplored
> How she presides over imbeciles.

A poet may take pride in his deliberate ignorance of old myths because, with that ignorance, he has the power—inspired by the moon—to create new ones; but he is ashamed that this same "queen of ignorance" rules the feeble-minded, the part of the population or of a man which is incapable of any knowledge. Stevens suggests that the really disturbing possibility underlying this shame is that man's grotesque, imbecilic, unconscious mind may be not only the capital but also the whole of his interior world, his self.

Stevens' first piece of advice is to conquer the shame by a bold entry into "that interior world"; then, to face the imbecilic character of that interior world, recognize the impossibility of reading its embryonic mind; and, in the same bold spirit, to recognize that this grotesque embryonic mind expresses itself in a public "absolute" way "within/The boulevards of the generals," as well as in an incommunicable, relative way in each man's private dream world. The image of the private grotesque is one of breathing; and, coming right after "The Pure Good of Theory," it suggests that, when Stevens wrote "a nature that is grotesque within/The boulevards of the generals," he had in mind the lines in the preceding poem: "Even breathing is the beating of time, in kind:/A retardation of its battering,/A horse grotesquely taut." He seems to have in mind an equestrian statue, a piece of public dream-work, like that of General du Puy in "Notes toward a Supreme Fiction."

"A Word with José Rodriguez-Feo" concludes by expanding this image of grotesque, imbecilic, public dream-work into a global, more *deliberately* vulgar, and therefore a more completely imagined image: "The sun comes up like news from Africa." Since all appearance is received unconsciously, it is all public property; and the fact that it is vulgarized by unimaginative men does not prevent the imaginative man from making of it what he can. One should note how much more easily Stevens' imagination is able to stomach and even digest the vulgar than it had been ten years earlier.

"Paisant Chronicle" recapitulates, briefly, the argument of "Examination of the Hero in a Time of War," emphasizing again the ordinary and sedentary aspect of the major man. But, whereas the hero in "Examination" (XV) might have been studying the wallpaper in his bedroom or the lemons on the table in his kitchen, the hero in "Paisant Chronicle" is publicly available for anyone to see, "seated in a café." The public aspect is emphasized, as in the other poems of this group.

"Sketch of the Ultimate Politician" is another "marker" poem —a poem that Stevens inserted at the end of a sequence of poems which, in this case, have a prominent social or political aspect. Stevens treats his ultimate politician with a respect quite different from that in "The politicians playing cards" in "The Glass of Water," a poem published nine years earlier. The ultimate politician is more like a poet than a vote-getter or a social engineer. A dreamer and a builder, he is most of all a man who can hear "Words that come out of us like words within,/That have rankled for many lives and made no sound." He is, then, the opposite of X in "The Creations of Sound" who does not say "ourselves" in syllables "rising in speech we do not speak." The ultimate politician revives the interrupted mythopoetic power of our past, a power which expresses itself in a dream of our future but which, in this politician's perspicacity, expresses a life that is already "beside us." As in "Crude Foyer" and in "Wild Ducks," *there* turns out to be *here*, if only we would stop thinking or trying to live in other lives. Or, as Stevens says in "Imagination as Value," an essay written at about the same time as "Sketch," "A generation ago we should have said that the imagination is an aspect of the conflict between man and nature. Today we are more likely to say that it is an aspect of the conflict between man and organized society" (NA 150).

The difference between calling a poet "X" (in "The Creations of Sound") and calling a flyer "This man" (in "Flyer's Fall") is that of a public versus a private concern. In "Flyer's Fall" a different kind of anger is expressed, one more personal than satirical: "This man escaped the dirty fates." "Flyer's Fall" is the first of a group of poems, ending with "Two Versions of the Same Poem," which express a degree of personal feeling that is unusual in Stevens. It is almost as if Stevens systematically focused in on the problem of myth-making, beginning with the sequence ending with "Crude Foyer," which treated the problem in a general way; concluding that *there* is *here*; proceeding to test that hypothesis in the social or political realm and then in the personal world.

"Flyer's Fall" provides a neat transition by carrying over the subject of war from the first poem of the preceding group, "Reptitions," and by repeating the most far-reaching conclusion of "The Pure Good of Theory," "We believe without belief, beyond belief." "Flyer's Fall" brings this public subject matter and this important belief about belief into the realm of personal feelings. For a myth must have not only a definite status, both in thought and in society, but also a personality. In the group of poems from "Flyer's Fall" to "Two Versions," Stevens' imagination moves in a direction opposite to that in the preceding group; now he is moving from the private toward the public, rather than from the public toward the private. He recognizes that he must be clear about the personal roots of his myth, even though, or even because, his myth is in itself impersonal.

It is hard not to read "Jouga" and "Debris of Life and Mind" from a psychoanalytic point of view. "Jouga" finds the physical world "tonight" meaningless except as the intercourse of a beastly couple; and "Debris" describes the Proust-like situation of a man reliving his boyhood: his begging his mother to stay with him in his room at night, fearful of losing his daytime mastery over her ("when the sky is so blue") and his conjuring up an image of her as a prostitute ("It is from this/That a bright red woman will be rising/And, standing in violent golds, will brush her hair."). The boy's mother brushes her hair in her own bedroom, and the violent golds suggest that her nighttime obedience to the boy's father has been bought. The boy's mastery in daytime is poetic and cannot be bought: "When the sky is so blue, things sing themselves." And the man has the somewhat uncertain satisfaction that what he gave his mother will outlast what his father paid her ("She will listen/And feel that her color is a meditation,/The most gay and yet not so gay as it was.") because he has given her both the color of her prostitution and that color as a meditation, subduing its gaiety but at the same time insuring its permanence. According to this reading of the poems, the last two lines of "Jouga" ("And after a while, when Ha-eé-me has gone to sleep,/A great jaguar running will make a little sound") suggest that after his parents have had intercourse, the little but imaginative son will show his great but as-yet-unrecognized strength. The figure is a combination of that in "Poetry Is a Destructive Force" and that in the last two lines of "Montrachet-le-Jardin."

The degree to which "Jouga" and "Debris" knit themselves into the whole fabric of Stevens' imagery and thought is as remarkable as the intensity of the feeling of personal reference that they convey. This double effect seems to be intentional. Each poem is a reversible coat that can be worn inside out or outside in with equal credibility. If the general theme of *Transport to Summer* is *"there* is *here,"* then on the personal or psychoanalytic side it means quite literally that the cosmos, so little of which is close and warm, is one's deepest psychic drama. But "Jouga" and "Debris" actually move in the opposite direction, from the life of the unconscious mind toward "the wind and the sea," "a great jaguar," and the color of meditation.

"Description without Place" emphasizes this movement outward from the unconscious to the mythical by the example in Part I of "this green queen," which in Part II is called "this queen or that,/The lesser seeming original in the blind/Forward of the eye that, in its backward, sees/The greater seeming of the major mind." This outward movement reaches its *theoretical* limit in Part III where so complete a change is accomplished that "we are content,/In a world that shrinks to an immediate whole,/That we do not need to understand, complete/Without secret arrangements of it in the mind." Part IV, the middle part of the poem, gives contrasting examples of near approaches by individuals (Nietzsche and Lenin) to this complete transformation. The last three parts treat the matter in terms derived from the Bible—the column in the desert, the dove, Revelation, and John I—but their import is that "seeming," or "description without place," is first of all unconscious, "a sense/To which we refer experience, a knowledge/Incognito" (Part V); therefore, it is "revelation," "a text we should be born that we might read"; and therefore "the theory of the word for those/For whom the word is the making of the world" (Part VI).

The last three parts of the poem are a recapitulation of the first three parts in terms of the word more than those of idealistic epistemology; and the Biblical language, like the "green queen" image, is used in what is for Stevens an unusually explicit and accepting way. Stevens seemingly feels freer now to use the language of the belief it is so necessary for him to reject: the belief of his mother's family, the Zellers. But, again, he uses a language that has deep personal associations in a deliberately new way. For instance, the striking figure in the last three lines of the poem—"what we say of the future must portend,/Be alive with its own seemings, seeming to be/Like rubies reddened by rubies reddening"—contains all the personal sexual reference one might want to read into it, if one reads it as an extension of the figure of the "bright red woman" in "Debris." At the same time this figure unites the Biblical and the phenomenological implications of the central conclusion of the poem: "Description is revelation": it is insightful, as Biblical prophecy was, seeing the future already accomplishing itself deeply, hiddenly in the present, and as modern phenomenology is, seeing the real present moment as a form of experience of which we are not conscious but which is "a sense/To which we refer experience." The more personal aspects of the poem—the psychoanalytic and the Biblical—are absorbed into and used up in its phenomenological import.

"Two Tales of Liadoff" is "Sketch of the Ultimate Politician" in more personal terms. Liadoff is a named person (as Nietzsche and Lenin are in "Description"); one can listen to his music and try to hear the things Stevens says happen to him. And the things that happen to him in this poem—"the whole return/From thought," "his body smothered him," "the instant to perceive"— have not only an intimate subjective feeling, but also, as their occasion, a folk-tale-like occurrence in village life. This occurrence is not in one family; there are men, women, and children. But the "townsmen" have a familial unity and intensity about them which makes "what they said" sharable as "The fantastic fortune of fantastic blood"; theirs is a smothering inarticulate need to perceive and express as precisely as a piano, their most expansive and explosive experiences. Liadoff sees and hears them on their wordless way up and on their wordy way down; and, by entering into both aspects of their need and their frustration, he perceives his oneness with them and so is able to express it in his music (Liadoff collected folk music and used folk themes in his own music). Stevens apparently felt a resemblance between Liadoff's deliberate transmutation of "archaic" material and his own of Biblical language in "Description." In both cases Stevens felt a recognition of familial roots, of "the fantastic fortune of fantastic blood."

"Analysis of a Theme" analyzes what is not so much a folk theme, such as Liadoff used, as a theme in a story improvised for one small child. But children's stories, even idiosyncratic ones, share with folk tales and the tales of the Bible a quality which, to Stevens, submerged the clearly unbelievable in the familial and in the familiar. In this poem he explains that such monsters as three-legged giraffes are met with on the way between the conscious world and Freud's inversion of Plato's myth of the cave. What was most real to Freud was the part of the self in which all the repressed parts of one's life continue their "ugly, subconscious time, in which/There is no beautiful eye/And no true tree." In the over-all spatial scheme of the metaphor there is "the conscious world" of clouds in the sky, the subterranean world of "ugly subconscious time," and, in between, "in time's middle deep," a realm of immaterial, nameless, "bright-ethered things," "Pure coruscations, that lie beyond/The imagination, intact/And unattained." "Middle deep" and "bright-ethered" recall the "fire-feinting sea" in "Esthetique du Mal," and what is quite possibly Santayana's realm of essences. Again, Stevens has carefully rooted his clearly unbelievable myth in the action of the blood, the unconscious mind.

"Late Hymn from the Myrhh-Mountain" is the first of Stevens' poems to contain a place-name from his childhood. "Myrhh-Mountain" is identified as Neversink, a mountain near Reading, Pennsylvania, where Stevens grew up. Having worked out a rationale for exposing the roots of his myth, he felt free to use names with deep personal associations. But, again, the name works two ways: both downward into his own life and outward into the public fabric of his poetry as a whole. Like Chocorua, Neversink has a shadow that is ultimately the shadow of night, winter, death, and "an external world." As the name suggests, such a shadow is an instance of the domination of black. "Late Hymn" describes a movement toward "ugly, subconscious time"— the opposite direction from the one taken in "Analysis."

A little of the deliberate nonsense of "Analysis" is carried over into the first words of "Late Hymn": "Unsnack your snood, madonna." Stevens uses the word "snood" only twice: here and in "The Rock," in the line, "The magnum wreath of summer, time's autumn snood." In both poems the snood is the last light covering of the bare earth before the winter night removes all disguises. Madonna, or my lady, is not quite a "long-haired Plomet" (planet plus comet); but she is addressed in a saucy, intimate way, as if she were a close relative, without diminishing her qualifications as a mate for "an external world." Her snood, unsnacked, will be "a shape left behind," the last evidence of the "uncertain love" of spring, "the knowledge of being" of summer. The snood has diamonds in it, the love and knowledge compressed and cut to bits of solid, shining artificial certainty; but their solidity and their artificiality demand one last act of love and knowledge: "Take the diamonds from your hair and lay them down." The approaching shadow is a lover and a knower that turns the gay color of the mother in "Debris" into its opposite, and erases all possible rancor or desire.

If the "madonna" of "Late Hymn" could be anyone from the human mother of "Debris" to mother earth, she has an anonymity similar to the "bright-ethered things" of "Analysis." In "Man Carrying Thing," this anonymity is carried to an extreme that permits Stevens to state one of his most famous beliefs: "The poem must resist the intelligence/Almost successfully." A nameless thing, or a thing with a name so personal (like "Neversink") that it is unknown to most readers, is something one cannot think about. So a "brune figure" has a color one is almost loath to look up in a dictionary; one would rather let the sound suggest the color. And "The thing he carries" is one giant step farther along on the way toward complete unintelligibility. Whatever "the bright obvious" at the end of the poem may be (one is reminded of the diamonds the madonna was told to lay down at the end of "Late Hymn"), one is more gratified by its and our having endured the storm of "our thoughts all night" than frustrated by any failure to identify it. Indeed, the gratification is so fine that the frustration falls away; and, as one of a group of personal poems, "Man Carrying Thing" makes sure of the fact that, whatever dark drama may toil at the heart of one's myth, it will finally be only perceived and not understood.

After enduring the snowflake-like thoughts all night in "Man Carrying Thing," one can shrug them off as "tinsel" in "Pieces" and concentrate on the wind that brought them and then ran away. This wind will never be "bright" or "obvious" or "motionless in cold." It is the irrational, inhuman "will of wills" (*CP* 480) that sustains the dark drama in one's heart, but it is at the same time "a person at night,/A member of the family."

The combination of the personal and the mythical is made more explicit in the first words of "A Completely New Set of Objects": "From a Schuylkill in mid-earth there come emerging/ Flotillas." "A Schuylkill" makes it clearly not *the* Schuylkill; unlike "Neversink," "Schuylkill" is a name most readers know. That it is the river in Stevens' home town need not be known, any more than it need be known that the rivers mentioned at the end of the poem have some significance in the early American history of Stevens' family. The big river, an extension of the wind image in "Pieces," extends the import of that image in two directions: the shapes of one's internal drama are carried up into public view—into poems—by the same current that sustains the drama; and beneath that current's tributaries (in a mythical psychological, not an actual geographical sense) "the fathers of the makers may lie and weather." The fathers of the makers, then, are also able to weather the storm of thoughts, as almost unknowable prototypes and archetypes. In this respect they are like "Again," the "ever-never-changing same," "the diva dame," in "Adult Epigram," or like "madonna" in "Late Hymn."

"Two Versions of the Same Poem" (first published in *Transport to Summer*), which seems to mark the end of the group of personal poems, takes the over-all metaphor of "A Completely New Set of Objects" and expands it into, first, a metaphor of a sleeping body in the center of the sea whose beating heart is "a strength that tumbles everywhere," ruining reason but pushing its conceptions toward realization. Second, old John Zeller sees the same phenomenon as an effort of neo-Platonic or Santayanaesque essences to escape their deadly origins. In both cases the ancestral body is told to sleep on undisturbed by the consequences of its ever-creative life or its ever-destructive death. As a conclusion to the group of personal poems, "Two Versions" expresses Stevens' deep sense of being at peace with the personal origins of his poetry, however turbulent the way may be from that origin to any particular poem.

Now, Stevens can openly speak of his myth, in "Men Made Out of Words," as "the sexual myth." At the same time, this power to call things by their right names turns his attention to words as such, as the title indicates. The next two poems, "Thinking of a Relation between the Images of Metaphor" and "Chaos in Motion and Not in Motion," follow almost mechanically from his remarks about language in "The Noble Rider and the Sound of Words": "Take the statement by Bateson that a language, considered semantically, evolves through a series of conflicts between the denotative and the connotative forces in words; between an asceticism tending to kill language by stripping words of all association and a hedonism tending to kill language by dissipating their sense in a multiplicity of associations (*NA* 13). "Thinking of a Relation" illustrates the extreme of denotation; "Chaos," that of connotation.

Most of the poems that follow are among Stevens' very best poems, and one of the marks of their excellence is their transparent yet moving language. They hardly require explication. The equilibrium between the imagination and reality, between denotation and connotation, is so precise that neither force dominates; and the two therefore have the greatest freedom to interpenetrate each other. This interpenetration is, of course, the final and most essential characteristic of a convincing myth.

"The House Was Quiet and the World Was Calm" finds the nicest balance between the denotative single-mindedness of "Thinking" (which kills "the dove") and the connotative chaos of "Chaos" (which results in Ludwig Richter's having "nothing more to think about"). The title of "The House Was Quiet and the World Was Calm" is repeated in its complete form twice in the poem; and, once again, the two parts are taken up separately for fuller exposition. The poem moves toward a oneness of reader, book, and summer night without violating the distinction between the house and the world, leading both the reader *in* the poem and the reader *of* the poem to a fuller and finer sense of the interpenetration of the calm (but not necessarily quite quiet) world and the quiet (but not necessarily quite calm) house. The man-made house and book, and the natural man and night are brought to this interpenetration by the intent posture of the man and by the relaxed posture of the rest of the world. The man's leaning is the precise angle of inclination to permit him to enter the calm world without disturbing it—to balance its rest, and not to upset that balance.[3]

Similarly, in "Continual Conversation with a Silent Man" a sense of equilibrium between earth and sky, reality and imagination, is so delicate that the reader of the poem can hear "the sound/Of things and their motion: the other man,/A turquoise monster moving round." The justice of this perception is so self-evident that an effort to read into it the personal situation in "Debris of Life and Mind" or the social situation in "The Creations of Sound" is both unnecessary and irrelevant. The personal and the social are completely absorbed and used up.

Even a more explicitly social situation shows itself to be amenable to this balanced treatment, as in "A Woman Sings a Song for a Soldier Come Home." This poem can be read as Hemingway's "Soldier's Home" with a happy ending. The soldier in the poem, unlike Hemingway's, does not lose anything because he talks about the weather with a man "So much a part of the place, so little/A person" that the latter might as well be "the other man" of "Continual Conversation." Even the worlds of war and peace can interpenetrate under these conditions, and the fictive hero can become the real so simply that the reader is hardly aware of it as a transformation.

Then, as if confident that social themes are no longer a real threat to him, Stevens returns to the theme of "The Creations of Sound" in "The Pediment of Appearance," treating the mid-forties pursuit of "the savage transparence" with a lightness and a justice that sounds almost happy compared with his treatment of X in "The Creations of Sound." And, if he can balance out the anger he felt for social problems, then why not also the fear he felt for personal ones? So, in "Burghers of Petty Death" he places the death of parental figures in "an imperium of quiet" that is only a little less his own quiet than is that in "The House Was Quiet and the World Was Calm." The figure of the poet in "Burghers" is "wasted" and his music is "blank" and "final," but the leaning reader in "The House" was not said to be either calm or quiet. The two figures reach toward each other and touch in the metaphor of release and fusion in "Human Arrangement," the word "Arrangement" fusing the sounds of the words "rain" and "change." Evening rain connotes release from the day's work, and yet it also binds one, as does its sound, "which does not change." And then, out of this tension between binding and release there rises "an imagined wooden chair," an image of both intention and fixity much like that of the leaning reader in "The House." The chair of both rain and change presides over an imperium (the chair is called "curule") that fuses the worlds of "The House" and "Burghers."

Perhaps in the next poem, "The Good Man Has No Shape," the poet was overconfident since he takes a theme before which he usually hesitated: that the theory of poetry is the theory of life. Anger and bitterness rise up irrepressibly, and the tone becomes flippant and sophomoric. But "The Red Fern" restores the balance. The impossibility of the many apprehending the shape of "The Good Man"—the *one* that the *many* really need as a new Adam—is removed by transposing the image into one that is both cosmic and everyday: the sunrise. The "physical fix of things" is not a shape but a point of focus, what Stevens calls in "Notes Toward a Supreme Fiction" a "first idea," and even an infant can perceive it.

"From the Packet of Anacharsis" is a little exercise in the expansion and contraction of connotation to illustrate a central doctrine: "In the punctual centre of all circles white/Stands truly." Essentially, the same doctrine underlies "The Dove in the Belly." The image in the title is one of maternity, as in "Holiday in Reality": "The flowering Judas grows from the belly or not at all . . . Spring is umbilical or else it is not spring." The toy egg out of which all the connotative excellence in the world is hatched is the poverty-stricken singularity of the dove in "Thinking of a Relation between the Images of Metaphor"; but that singularity contains it all. "Mountains Covered with Cats" looks at that poverty-stricken singularity through Freud's eye, "the microscope of potency." The result is of course ironical: "the invalid personality" never is what it is, and so it is radically more fecund than nature which repeats itself with infinite monotony.

In "The Prejudice Against the Past" Stevens returns to the two-part harmony of the connotative and the denotative that was so successful in "The House" and in "Continual Conversation." "Day" is so singular for children that it has no article, definite or indefinite; therefore it has for them the simple, all-inclusive fertility of a friend—like a cart, which carries everything, including the sun and the sky, or "a very big hat," which covers everything, because it covers the eyes. "Aquiline pedants," whose eagle brows are designed to shield their eyes from the sun, take the hat for a detached brow with the same function: a relic of the mind which confines itself to reflection, rather than direct perception. And by the same token, "aquiline pedants" take the cart, which receives only direct impressions, for a relic of the heart. As *detachable* containers, hat and cart can only be relics and parts of oneself; as true and inseparable equivalents and friends, hat and cart are as singular and whole and perpetual as "day."

In "Extraordinary References" the children's three-in-one friend (day, cart, hat) is simplified still more into three ribbons in the child's plaited hair. But this simplification contains a further complication: the mother who ties the ribbons revives, in tying them, the painful memory of her husband's death in war, and that painful memory comes to her at first harmlessly in the memory that the child's great-grandfather fought Indians (who perhaps wore their hair braided). But the child's prejudice against the past, her simple identification with the sun which at its rising streams as barbarously as the child's unplaited hair, helps the mother to have peace. The act of tying ribbons in the child's hair composes all that is wild and painful, just as the noun "hair-ribbons"—after connoting or referring to several extraordinary people, places, and things—gathers those extraordinary references into one ordinary denotation of one person, place, and thing.

In the next poem, "Attempt to Discover Life," Stevens again takes confidence in his power to compose the painful past into the peaceful present; and he deals both starkly and sympathetically with another parental pair. This poem contrasts revealingly with both "Burghers" and the early "Floral Decorations for Bananas." The early poem has the brassy note of the all-concealing, all-rejecting dandy; "Burghers" simplifies the situation too much by treating the parental figures as last leaves. "Attempt" does neither. The parental figures are explicitly dead, explicitly hungry for life; and life is neither simply and obscurely obscene bananas nor simply and cosmically the black tree. Life is "fomentations of effulgence" rising from versicolored roses. Present life crowds out the dead, who leave behind all their substance, all their power to live, in the form of an infinitesimal tip, as if to thank the living for the privilege of only *smelling* life. This tip puts the situation in "Extraordinary References" in plain terms of pesos and centavos—the bottom-most meaning of *"This spring after the war,/In which your father died, still breathes for him/ And breathes again for us a fragile breath."* But the breath is not nearly so fragile as the father. It is ironical that Freud's ghost in "Mountains" may understand how truly the impotent dead "had not been what they were," because their lives proliferated radically while they were alive, and that therefore they were the opposite of impotent. But the irony works both ways: once dead, a personality is no more potent than a centavo.

"A Lot of People Bathing in a Stream" is the first of three poems newly published in *Transport to Summer*; it and one more poem from the fall of 1946 constitute a terminus to the group of poems that begins with "Men Made Out of Words"—poems devoted primarily to the problem of the one and the many as it appears in efforts to balance the connotative and the denotative tendencies in language. "A Lot of People" simply juxtaposes a proliferation of forms into the grotesque (stopping short of Ludvig Richter's chaos) with a changeless containment of those forms. The forms are humans, the place of proliferation is "the sun-filled water" of a stream, and the place of changeless containment is "the frame of the house." This sharp contrast prepares the reader for the subtler growths, containments, and decays of "Credences of Summer," Stevens' most extended treatment of the problem of the one and the many. Summer at its summit, at the moment when it has become "the barrenness/Of the fertile thing that can attain no more," contains all the life of the year, all twelve months, the rock of winter and nothingness, "spring's infuriations," and the decay that follows the maximum. "The personae of summer," the old non-reader who "Absorbs the ruddy summer" and "fulfils his age," the twelve months like twelve princes, the "cock bright" who announces and watches the decay—these personae are finally described in terms that recall the human figures in "A Lot of People." "Credences" takes a giant step toward transforming those human figures into real personae of a real myth.[4] And "A Pastoral Nun" and "The Pastor Caballero" are two small steps in the same direction, or rather a hop and a skip before the mighty leap in "Notes Toward a Supreme Fiction," which comes nearer to genuine, winged flight than anything else in Stevens.

"A Pastoral Nun" applies the lesson of "Credences" (the summary power of "the last day of a certain year") to a single lifetime: "Finally, in the last year of her age,/Having attained a present blessedness,/She said poetry and apotheosis are one." This oneness contains the manyness of "an immense activity, . . . As of a general being or human universe." Such a human universe includes not only the personae of a cosmic drama but the smallest, most mundane things, like the hat of "The Pastor Caballero." In such an inclusion the hat's brim acquires a grandiloquence that makes it go well with "the green flauntings of the hours of peace." These last two poems are symmetrical with "Thinking" and "Chaos" at the beginning of the group of poems devoted to the one and the many, denotation and connotation. The denotative contraction of "Thinking" is repeated, but in a far more fertile way, by "The Pastor Caballero"; and the connotative expansion of "Chaos" is repeated, but in a far more orderly way, by "A Pastoral Nun."

"Notes Toward a Supreme Fiction" stands by itself as the myth complete, or as nearly complete as Stevens could imagine it. The poem gathers together the four concerns which characterize the rest of the poems in *Transport to Summer*: there is here, the public aspect of myth, the personal aspect, and the balance between connotation and denotation.

"Notes" begins with a formal dedication, to Stevens' friend, Henry Church—and thus explicitly emphasizes at the outset the concern that is new and peculiar to *Transport*: open references to Stevens' personal life. Stevens apparently felt that if he seriously believed that "there is here," his myth must be clearly rooted in his personal life, however public that myth might become and however much it might have to struggle to maintain a balance between the denotative and the connotative tendencies in language. This troubled and belated effort toward confession follows quite simply from the adagium at the beginning of this chapter: "Life is an affair of people, not of places. But for me life is an affair of places and that is the trouble." The cosmic connotations of words describing landscapes came naturally and comparatively easily to Stevens; the social connotations, with difficulty. By the same token, when he reversed the direction, contracting the meanings toward denotation, still lifes came naturally; personal confessions, with difficulty. And, since he believed that a balance between connotation and denotation, imagination and reality, the one and the many can be achieved only by a movement back and forth between the two poles, he had to try to confess, painfully difficult as it was.

The dedication to Henry Church emphasizes the central, peaceful transparence between two friends; and the advice to ephebe, which begins the poem proper, assumes a similar transparence between the teacher and ephebe and between both of them and the physical world. The supreme fiction must be abstract in the sense that it must begin (as "Notes" does) with pure denotation and therefore with a return to pure ignorance. Pure denotation is simply a pointing gesture; it is a refusal to name the thing pointed at, because a name such as "sun" connotes all the suns in the experience of the speaker and the listener. Our world is full of suns, the different suns of different times and places; and this omnipresence and immortality tends to make the sun into a god. As a supreme *fiction*, a poem must begin with a nameless image, a first idea, that is isolated or *abstracted* from a world which, inasmuch as it is named, is oppressively god-like.

Such a completely named world is like an apartment house, and the ennui of living in it drives one away toward a purely denotative hermit life for refreshment and then back again for completion. These motives and these movements are described in Parts I, II, and III of "It Must Be Abstract." Parts IV, V, and VI develop the absolute otherness of the first idea and the consequent difficulty of yoking it with the tame half of a metaphor in order to keep it at the heart of the poem but not name it. The tame half of the metaphor is a persona, minimally human, "the giant of the weather." Parts VII, VIII, and IX take up and reject the romantic tendency to be satisfied with a union between the human and the natural—as, for example, in sex or in ocean-bathing—without having gone through the saintly labor of giving birth to the giant. This romantic evasion misleads those who indulge in it into thinking of themselves as gods, a mistake as great as the one ephebe was warned against in Part I: that of naming and thereby deifying the world. What the romantics were most consciously evading was "reason's click-clack," scientific thought, which makes one so aware of his alienation from nature that he cannot realistically imagine that it emanates effortlessly from him, or him from it. Reason and "the infected past" intervene, and "the major man"—the man who is as interpenetrated by nature as the giant of the weather is interpenetrated by man—must be as much a child of reason and the past as he is a child of nature.

Major man is not the tame half of a metaphor, however, as is the giant of the weather; major man is a first idea; indeed, he is a first idea of a first idea, a further abstraction of the abstract idea of common man (using "abstract" in the special, visual sense expounded in Part I). Part X offers a taming image for this wildest of ideas, an image of a cumulative human figure "in his old coat,/His slouching pantaloons, beyond the town,/Looking for what was, where it used to be." His look and his looking are much like those of the soldier in "A Woman Sings a Song for a Soldier Come Home" (perhaps wearing fatigues or a worn-out combat uniform); and in the epilogue at the end of "Notes" there appears this line: "How simply the fictive hero becomes the real." The figure of the soldier come home embodies both the chieftain's sense of the angry upshot of the past and the rabbi's sense of the past as an understandable congealed thing; he also contains a deeply painful need to return to an ignorant, purely denotative perception of nature. And these qualities are what the common man shares with the major man, for they are what the real soldier shares with the ideal poet.[5] Major man is the ideal poet.

"It Must Be Abstract" aims at two kinds of singularity: the purely denotative first idea and the cumulative figure of common man. Both of these singularities tend to be changeless; and a supreme fiction (an ideal poem), if it adheres to reality, must change. Change means manyness; and "It Must Change," the second major division of "Notes," reverses the direction of "It Must Be Abstract," breeding out of the supreme singularities *many*, ever-new, ever-changing "particulars of rapture."

In Part I of "It Must Change" first ideas (violets, doves, girls, bees, hyacinths) repeat themselves; they do not seem to change. In Part II, such a universe of changeless first ideas would have a ridiculously representative form of government in which the present *named* representative of all the bees, the president of them, would lay down the law of the immortality of bees for all time. But for each individual bee (or lover), its appearance on the scene is not a recurrence but a new beginning. In Part III, a truly changeless, named executive would be like a bronze statue of a general which in the course of centuries (the example is a general of the Crusades) would come to seem absurd and finally become rubbish. In Part IV, change, or rather our sense of change, originates in the union of a first idea with an imagined, composite figure for which the first idea was the original germ. Spring is always fresh because it begins the sequence that ends in winter; if spring did not follow winter, one would not be aware of its freshness. The same could be said for the dead samenesses of parts I, II, and III: their deadness makes one aware of the newly living things that went into their composition. Similarly, in Part V, the deadness of the planter makes the continued blooming and bearing of his plantation vividly new. But, even in his lifetime, he labored to grow fruit in a tension between a real womblike fruitfulness that he remembered from his childhood and an ideal genital fruitfulness which he imagined "to the South." That tension was a positive light, one in which the fruits of his labor were always new to him. For "An unaffected man in a negative light/Could not have borne his labor, nor have died/Sighing that he should leave the banjo's twang."

In Part VI, subhuman nature in itself, the planter's oranges in themselves, or even the more obviously aspiring birds have no dream, no ideal of paradise. Subhuman creatures look down, rather than up; they demand and receive their intimate identity ("Be thou me") with lower forms of life, with their origins. Therefore, they do not live in the planter's positive tension; and the wild world they live in and feed on but do not cultivate—the world of which they are themselves indissolubly a part—does not change for them, is never new for them. Their world, unlike the planter's world which he constantly labors to bring closer to his paradisal ideal, will end with the death of each individual or with the extinction of each species.

As in "It Must Be Abstract" VII, "It Must Change" VII turns to the romantic evasion of idealistic artistic labor—an evasion which, again, originates in experiences like sex which lead one to say, "We have not the need of any paradise." But such experiences also lead one to make the foolish assumption of Nanzia

Nunzio, in Part VIII, that one can strip oneself of all artifice, as if it were merely ornamental, and unite oneself with a past perfection of art, presumably in order to give birth to future perfections of art. Nanzia Nunzio tries to reduce herself to the dreamless condition of the birds in Part VI, but as Ozymandias remarks at the end of Part VIII, she cannot: "the bride/Is never naked. A fictive covering/Weaves always glistening from the heart and mind."

Part IX explores the wiser assumption that the fully constituted fiction is always in a language which is, in other contexts, as dead as Latin but which in poetry is compounded with "the lingua franca et jocundissima"—what he was later to call "the eye's plain version . . . the vulgate of experience": the nameless first idea. Each extreme by itself is gibberish. The poem has a true, changeful life only in its movement back and forth between the two extremes, or in a compounding of them.

Part X sums up "It Must Change" by picturing the disreputable-looking cumulative figure of "It Must Be Abstract" (X) sitting on a park bench watching the west wind fill the water of the lake with "artificial things," "changing essences"—first ideas becoming filled-out fictions. And since he, and not the physical west wind, is responsible for these ever-fresh transformations, the poet in him can see that he is looking at himself. Or, since he is a cumulative figure, through him one can look at oneself. By constantly rubbing that glass clear of past associations, the ideal poet can ensure ever-fresh receptions of first ideas and, having all the time in the world, make poems of them.

"It Must Give Pleasure" begins, by rejecting in Part I another form of vulgar changelessness (as did Part I in "It Must Be Abstract" and "It Must Change")—the Vulgate Latin version of the Bible prepared by St. Jerome. The inescapable need for a dream of paradise emphasized in "It Must Change" makes a widely enjoyed record of such a dream a relevant example of an attempt "to compound the imagination's Latin" with "the vulgate of experience." But Jerome's Vulgate has the fault of arresting the fictions of an enormous society for a great length of time. Although the pleasure that that society enjoys, en masse, in singing the words of the Bible "at exact, accustomed times" is a great one, it is "a facile exercise" because the true pleasure of myth-making is in starting, constantly, with nameless first ideas

("To find of sound the bleakest ancestor"). And the true pleasure given by any myth, any supreme fiction, is given by the changeful first ideas that remain ever freshly alive within it.

The reader is "shaken" by these first ideas, and so the blue woman (the rational woman) of Part II tries to prevent the growth of the sexual myth out of the first ideas she receives while at her window from a moonlight night. Her effort takes the form of insisting that the color of the dogwoods remain precisely the "coral" that she sees it to be, but her effort defeats itself because "coral" is itself a fossil metaphor with an underground life of its own. The dogwood bush becomes, against her will, "A lasting visage in a lasting bush" which fills itself out with ugly frowning features; and it finally brings to the blue woman's mind a sexually disturbing and liberating dream-memory of her childhood, at the end of Part III.

The blue woman's mistake was to reason about her perceptions too soon—to force them into fixed categories before they had, with the difficulty of art, developed their own metaphorical tethers. The right way of proceeding is illustrated in Part IV, which begins with the last line of Part I, "We reason of these things with a later reason." The captain and Bauda are slow to marry, slow to fix their relationship, unlike Nanzia Nunzio and the blue woman. When the captain and Bauda do marry, they marry metaphors of each other, the sun and the hill: their essences are not named, nor is their relationship ever the fixed one of two named ideas put into a proposition.

Parts V and VI develop a more elaborate example: that of the Canon Aspirin and his sister. The Canon is involved in the most luxurious and sedative form of the Christian myth, but his sister deals with her daughters in an extremely attentive, ascetic way. The Canon and his sister represent the extremes of denotation and connotation, reality and imagination, first idea and full-blown myth. As brother and sister, they cannot marry; their relationship is given, natural, inescapable. But in its deeply pleasurable terms—the sister's "sensible ecstasy" in her care for her children; the "huge pathetic force" of the Canon's celibate, sacerdotal care for the same children—they are joined in a way that is as all-embracing as a marriage made in heaven. Again it is a nameless, metaphorical relationship, the children forming the taming half of the metaphor.

In Part VII the Canon's choice to include everything in "the whole,/The complicate, the amassing harmony" is seen to be too much a deductive, *imposed* order. Stevens wants to whittle that enormous superstructure down to its one essential, the fiction of an absolute, an angel—and otherwise to discover, not to invent, the order of his myth. This angel is like the giant of the weather in "It Must Be Abstract" (VI), except that the giant is minimally human while the angel is minimally superhuman.

In Part VIII, Stevens questions if the angel's powers of flight are not his, especially since the downward part of that flight is the more glorious. He concludes that those powers are his, meaning that—once he has achieved the essence of paradise, the fiction of an absolute—he is free to accept for his paradise *this* world, and himself as he is. The paradisal height of the angel's flight is useful only as a point of view (like that of the height of summer in "Credences") from which one can see the whole human and subhuman world in one joyous glance. And so, in Part IX, Stevens can find his own kind of sympathy with the undreaming birds of "It Must Change" (VI): he too can enjoy "mere repetitions," when he is sure he can also "Do all that angels can . . . enjoy like them,/Like men besides." In fact the enjoyment, the greatest mastery of repetitions, may be the chief distinguishing feature of major man, the ideal poet.

The climactic example of the enjoyment of repetitions in Part IX is

> the going round
> And round and round, the merely going round,
> Until merely going round is a final good,
> The way wine comes at a table in a wood.
>
> And we enjoy like men, the way a leaf
> Above the table spins its constant spin,
> So that we look at it with pleasure, look
>
> At it spinning its eccentric measure.

As the wine goes round, the men become like birds, with the difference that they also perceive the angelic eccentricity of the spinning of the leaf (cf. "Dutch Graves").

In Part X, the poet is drunk with the revolving wine of Part IX, and his final address to his fictive earthly paradise, whom he calls "Fat girl," has the elaborate civility of drunkenness. Fat girl is both the most ordinary of women and "the more than natural figure," "the more than rational distortion,/The fiction that results from feeling." But the poet looks forward to the day when the two aspects of fat girl, the fictive and the real, the irrational and the rational, will become one: "Until flicked by feeling, in a gildered street,/I call you by name, my green, my fluent mundo./You will have stopped revolving except in crystal." Then, contrary to the present situation, as it is described in "Esthetique du Mal" (XI), man shall be "At the centre of a diamond"; then he shall have achieved the essential prose with which to denote, with accurate names, the earthly paradise in which he lives. He will no longer need the eccentric, downward-spinning angel's point of view as a means to enjoy earthly repetitions; earthly revolving, compressed into transparent language, will seem to have stopped, and he will be satisfied.

The epilogue simply applies this lesson to the merging of a soldier's experience with that of the poet.

CHAPTER 4

The Auroras of Autumn and The Rock

I The Auroras of Autumn

"THE AURORAS OF AUTUMN" states the theme of the book of which it is the title poem: an abandonment of dreams of paradise and an acceptance of the windings of this world's appearance—not by choice, as in "It Must Give Pleasure" (VIII and IX), but of necessity because of the imminence of death. The poems from "Auroras" through "The Beginning" express, primarily, the ambiguous character of a compulsory acceptance of change. The next series of poems, from "The Countryman" through "Study of Images II," argues for a more or less positive acceptance of change. And finally, "An Ordinary Evening in New Haven," "Things of August," and "Angel Surrounded by Paysans" are examples of such an acceptance.

The snake image in Part I of "The Auroras of Autumn" asserts three qualities of the experience of autumn or old age: the sense of the coiled, of a skin that can be shed, and of something poisonous. Appearance is intricate, and it is also only a skin; but the body within the skin is a poisonous predator. The aurora borealis —seen as the serpent of appearance—is a withdrawal of the colors, deceptions, and dangers of life into a nest in the northern sky. Its ultimate poison is that man can't believe its withdrawal can ever be so complete that it becomes its opposite: a polar brightness in the midst of midnight, a complete happiness beyond life in the midst of death.[1] In Part II, disbelief in a heavenly afterlife is represented by the image of a white summer cabin on a beach, which slowly loses its whiteness with the coming of autumn. The aurora borealis "is always enlarging the change." In Part III, disbelief is tracked down to a memory of the transparent peace the mother gave us as children but which, after her death, seems to end as abruptly as if by the knock of a rifle-butt against the door. In Part IV, the father is represented as having given, and as still giving, the excitement implied by the rifle-butt against the door: the rapid changes of weather which are not so much dangerous as they are thrilling. In Part V, this changeable atmosphere brought by the father is dramatized as a kind of domestic masque "dubbing at tragedy." In VI, the more sinister qualities of this theatricality are developed until the tone of the poem is similar to that in Part I: "the scholar of one candle sees/An arctic effuigence flaring on the frame/Of everything he is. And he feels afraid."

Part VII entertains the question that was expressed as a poisonous disbelief in Part I: "These lights may finally attain a pole/In the midmost midnight and find the serpent there,/In another nest, the master of the maze." In Part VII, this disbelief passes from a question to a working hypothesis, according to which the master imagination, if it "leaps through us," must do so, not as our darkest destiny but as "slight caprice," as "Say, a flippant communication under the moon." Part VIII shows that, in this deliberately capricious character, imagination may be a principle of innocence. Then the lights of the aurora borealis are "An innocence of earth and no false sign/Or symbol of malice," and man can return to the peace the mother gives. In Part IX, the memory of the intense isolation and freedom of the rendez-vous of the mother and the child alone together in the night (the situation in "Debris") creates the imagination of disaster. But these two poles, the remembered beatitude and the imminent disaster, may be reversible and therefore identical: perhaps death, with no paradise beyond, may come "Almost as the tenderest and truest part" of innocence.

This identity of opposites is brought to its most tough-minded image at the end of Part X, the end of the poem: "a blaze of straw, in winter's nick." The paradise which in "Notes" could be accepted and then rejected, deliberately, on principle, must now be called by its right name—a memory of mother-and-child innocence; and the imminent disaster, winter or death, which now feels like a compulsory rejection of the mother-and-child paradise, must be seen to be a memory of the capricious judgments and excitements brought by the father that converted the mother into a harridan and the memory-hope of paradise into something both wilder and tenderer than the remembered mother-and-child innocence. "Auroras," after digging more deeply into the Proustian situation of "Debris," ends on an ambiguous note similar to that on which Whitman's "Out of the Cradle Endlessly Rocking" ends.

"Page from a Tale" develops this ambiguity in the image of Hans's *Südenlust*, beside a drift-fire on the frozen arctic sea—an image that proceeds directly from the one that ends "Auroras," "a blaze of straw in winter's nick." Hans can hear in the wind (the father's capricious judgment in "Auroras") the words of Yeats's dream of a Thoreauvian hermitage, and this imagination of opposites included in each other saves him from the fears and the grotesque fancies which blind and deafen the men on the ship to the tenderness within the harshness of the place. These men are like living dead men; and "Large Red Man Reading" develops that idea in the image of the delight that such men would take, once they were really dead, in the most ordinary and even painful ("the most coiled thorn") things of this world.

"This Solitude of Cataracts" expresses an attitude contrary to that expressed in "Large Red Man Reading": "the most coiled thorn," the endless changing of things on earth *is* painful and one wishes to escape it—not into the heavens with their "oscillations of planetary pass-pass" but into a deliberately artificial permanence. "In the Element of Antagonisms" hastens to reassert one of Stevens' most persistent beliefs: the life and death changes of this world are too mighty and too large for such a bronze or even golden permanence to last.

Unless, as in "In a Bad Time," the permanence is simply that of poverty—of the heart's strongest *need* for a permanent order. That need is the naked core of tragedy; that cannot die. To that nakedness, in "The Beginning," "the first tutoyers of tragedy/ Speak softly." These four poems together ("This Solitude," "In the Element," "In a Bad Time," and "The Beginning") clarify the meaning of the lines at the end of "Auroras" IX: disaster "may come tomorrow in the simplest word,/Almost as part of innocence, almost,/Almost as the tenderest and the truest part."

"The Countryman," a poem published for the first time in *The Auroras of Autumn*, was apparently inserted to mark the beginning of a group of poems devoted to a positive acceptance of change, the capricious weather of the father in "Auroras." Swatara is a river in the hills some miles west of Reading, Pennsylvania; its "swarthy name" suggests the darkest aspect of change. Nevertheless, the countryman, the ignorant unspeaking man of the place, needs to walk beside it, needs it as an unspeaking presence. But, if the countryman needs this swarthy movement, Stevens needs the opposite in "In the Element of Antagonisms." "The Ultimate Poem is Abstract" tries to come closer to a definition of the need for stasis and concludes that it is the need to enjoy the enormous sense of "this day" which one would have "at the middle." The troublesome writhing of the day is "an intellect/Of windings round and dodges to and fro . . . Not an intellect in which we are fleet." But the enormous sense does not wind and does not have to be fleet. Furthermore, as Stevens shows in "Bouquet of Roses in Sunlight," the enormous sense at the center (which tends to be "white" in *Auroras*) "exceeds all metaphor." A master of metaphor, the father in "Auroras" was an intellect that was fleet in the windings of the weather, both exciting and frightening; but the reader can exceed this rhetorical virtuosity in the simplest, most fundamental sense of things.

That fundamental sense of things, as it is intensified in "The Owl in the Sarcophagus," is divided into three aspects: sleep, peace, and "she that says/Goodby in the darkness." Sleep is "the whiteness that is the ultimate intellect" in life; peace is sleep's desired counterpart after death; and "she that says goodbye" is the sense of things quickened by their passing away from the immediate present into memory. Stevens calls her "the mother of us all,/The earthly mother and the mother of/The dead." She is a more merciful version of the harridan figure at the end of "Auroras" in that she makes the sequence—mother-and-child immediacy followed by disaster (death)—into a passionate form of knowledge. It is a way of knowing that is fleeter than that of the father in "Auroras," but it is as primitive as the self beneath the sense of self. To add another metaphor to Stevens' trio, it is as if the still folds of sleep and peace were the folds of space-time that science-fiction writers talk about—and as if "she that says goodbye" were the incredible speed of association and discrimination possible in sleep, achieved by tiny movements across the space-time warp, where the folds of sleep lie close to each other.[2] The intellect of the father in "Auroras" takes the long way around since he is an image of conscious thought seen as cosmic weather. His is an intellect in which man is not fleet ("The Ultimate Poem Is Abstract"); but the mother's is one in which man is.

"Saint John and the Back-Ache" associates "mind," or conscious thought, with force and pain, which are too slow to follow the moment-to-moment change in our sense of things. The female figure, "she that says goodbye" in "The Owl," is somewhat discarded by Saint John, who emphasizes that the present sense of things, or their presence (since he wants it to be external), is "not the woman, come upon,/Not yet accustomed." Such a figure, whether mistress or mother, is the Eve in this Eden of immediacy. The true knowledge of "the morality of the right sensation" (*NA* 58) is that of the serpent at the beginning of "Auroras."

In moving back and forth from hard-to-accept to easy-to-accept images of change and immediacy, Stevens appears to have worked his way into an accepting attitude that is almost surprising. It is not completely surprising because in "Auroras" and in "The Owl" he probed deeper into his personal past than ever before. Nevertheless, when in "Celle Qui Fût Héaulmiette" "she found a helping from the cold" in "Another American vulgarity," one may remember "The American Sublime," published fifteen years earlier, and wonder a little what has happened.

Examining the image of the cloud-shield in "Celle Qui," one finds the image of white central stillness met in "Bouquet of Roses" and in "The Owl," as well as its fluid or quickening aspect ("And yet with water running in the sun"). It is at this point that Stevens seems almost to reject the shield as too gaudy: "Entinselled and gilderlinged and gone,/Another American vulgarity." But the next four lines show that, if the grimmest aspects of one's personal past can be accepted, so can "another American vulgarity." Once Stevens could admit, in his poetry, that the vitality of his myth required clearly perceived personal roots, the capital of his imaginative *mundo* could be moved from Paris to Washington, D.C.

An image of solid white turning liquid is placed at the climax of the next poem, "Imago." As in "Celle Qui," Stevens is somewhat preoccupied with nationality; and Imago—if it is to have the power to lift not only post-war Britain, Germany, and France but also vulgar America—must be like "A glacier running through delirium."

"A Primitive Like an Orb" adds nothing new to Stevens' myth; its beauty lies in the carefully gradual way in which the giant is evoked, always just barely believable as a metaphor. "A Primitive" may be read as a modification of the last two lines of the preceding poem, "Imago": *"Lightly and lightly, O my land,/ Move lightly through the air again."* The giant rises lightly and delicately although he is enormous and all-powerful.

"A Primitive" might have been subtitled "Metaphor as Generation"; the next poem, "Metaphor as Degeneration" is a criticism of its own title. "Metaphor" extends the interpenetration of heaviness and lightness, which characterizes "A Primitive," into images of death and the imagination, and declares these two to be the necessary and sufficient constituents of all being. The point of the poem is that if any particular river, say Swatara, becomes the river of being—which in turn becomes the destructive-creative (death and the imagination) ocean—then how can this ever-expanding and finally-all-inclusive metaphor be a degeneration? Even as it is, without metaphor, the ever-changing flow of Swatara composes the black violets of death on its banks with the green mosses of the imagination that hang upon it.

Similarly, the disembodied "warmth and movement" of a woman characterize a summer day in "The Woman in Sunshine" without disturbing the integrity of the physical scene and without adding a hallucinatory "image in the air." All three of these poems, "A Primitive," "Metaphor," and "The Woman" substantiate the thesis of "Reply to Papini": "The way through the world/Is more difficult to find than the way beyond it." "The Bouquet," a more extended example of the same principle, emphasizes the ephemeral character of the metaphorical metamorphosis of a thing that is not only clearly seen for what it is but is also fully imagined for what it might be. It is a character like that of "she that says good-by" in "The Owl," and it is mentioned briefly in "A Primitive" (II). Most of the import of the poem is the usual one: that the unreal is most useful as a thing that makes the real more acute. But the last part of the poem suggests that the opposite is true, too: the single-minded soldier, who, in ignoring the bouquet knocks it over, throws all the metamorphoses of the bouquet into a realm of *vivid* unreality. It is not until such a solidly and alienly human being as the soldier is naturalized into the amenable element of the still-life, as the father and mother are in "The World Without Peculiarity," that the unreal and the real, imagination and death, can become "a single being, sure and true." "Our Stars Come from Ireland" goes one step further to say that the amenable element of nature, whether seen as still life or landscape, is made out of one's childhood self. The "whole habit of the mind" is changed in that making, but it is a change into what is perpetually childlike, perpetually morning.

That making can convert the "wild bitch" of autumn (the "hall harridan" of "Auroras") into a poor little girl in "Puella Parvula." But just as the making may rejuvenate or even apotheosize the maker, it may also be fatal, as in "The Novel." If the real is "made more acute by an unreal" ("The Bouquet"), acuteness at its extreme may be "the fatality of seeing things too well." Or, when the unreal is not a novel by Camus but rather the metaphors attendant on the fading of noon toward night, "what we think" (the unreal) "is never what we see," as "What We See Is What We Think" concludes. In the next poem, "A Golden Woman in a Silver Mirror," that unreality is not only not "the fatality of seeing things too well" but also the root of everything and therefore a means of ascending to an absolute that survives death, a "glittering crown,/Sound-soothing pearl and omni-diamond,/Of the most beautiful, the most beautiful maid/And mother." But, finally, as at the end of "The Bouquet," that degree of unreality does away with itself; so "The Old Lutheran Bells at Home," after being "the voices of the pastors calling," finally belong to the sextons "As they jangle and dangle and kick their feet."

The fatal or rejuvenating or apotheosizing powers of the imagination are all brought together and reduced to the ridiculousness of the question that "drowsy, infant, old men" ask of the sun—"Mother, my mother, who are you"—in "Questions Are Remarks." By contrast, the two-year-old grandson's question is a complete and sufficient statement: "Mother, what is that?" But in "Study of Images I" Stevens consoles himself with the fact that even the faded images of a drowsy infant old man can be sufficient "if images are all we have": "They can be no more faded than ourselves./The blood refreshes with its stale demands." "Study of Images II" continues the same meditation by asserting that the frequency of faded images is "more or less." There are none for the imminent dead winter of the self, but quite enough for the rest of life—for the pearly women like that of "A Golden Woman in a Silver Mirror."

"An Ordinary Evening in New Haven" is the first of a series of three poems placed at the end of *Auroras* as examples of a more or less positive acceptance of change. Published as a poem with eleven parts, twenty more parts were added later, leaving the original eleven interspersed among the final thirty-one. The original eleven are spaced out and grouped together to divide the final poem into six parts, which are numbered, in the final form, I-V, VI-X, XI-XV, XVI-XXI, XXII-XXVII, XXVIII-XXXI. Parts I-V deal with the inevitability of metaphor and with its inevitable convergence with and quickening of reality.[3] Parts VI-X emphasize the primary importance of the return from the extremes of metaphor to reality. Parts XI-XV show how the imagination that is alive with the real can make new heaven on earth, even in ordinary New Haven. Parts XVI-XXI explore the difficulties of imagining "this present" (New Haven) since it has never been done before ("the great poems of heaven and hell have been written and the great poem of the earth remains to be written" [*NA* 142]). The image of this present must be neither comic nor tragic but commonplace; it must break away from "the window," the already-constructed frames of perception, and find the center, "the radial aspect of this place." The image of this present must become one of "A naked being with a naked will," which is both the will of an individual man (the poet) and "the will of necessity, the will of wills." The two wills, "The two romanzas, the distant and the near,/Are a single voice in the boo-ha of the wind."

Parts XXII-XXVII make a modest beginning of the new myth of earth by asserting that it is "as momentous as the search for god"; by discarding the statue of Jove; and, starting with the poet's familiar figure of the hidalgo (life), by sketching in a new pair of archetypal parents, The Ruler of Reality and the Queen of Fact. Parts XXVIII-XXXI make a few final suggestions about the coincidence of the real and the unreal, the most interesting of which is in Part XXIX (originally Part XI), to the effect that the unreal is simply the real (New Haven, "the land of elm trees") "folded over, turned round." The poem ends with the emphasis that is characteristic throughout *The Auroras of Autumn*: "It is not in the premise that reality/Is a solid. It may be a shade that traverses/A dust, a force that traverses a shade."

"Ordinary Evening" concentrates on the moment of maximum change from light to dark, the moment of evening with its obvious resemblances to autumn. "Things of August" describes at length the life of the imagination at the moment before autumn. It is the moment after that height of summer described in "Credences of Summer"; and the weary desperation that it conceals is best expressed in the images in "Things" (X), images of the mother exhausted and the stamping father not quite yet arrived. "Things" carefully records both the inner emotional and the outer sensuous feel of this sad time of the year; Stevens is trying, as usual, to make the two sides show themselves to be as nearly identical as possible. The best parts are the "personal" ones—IV, VIII, and X—which use images of parental figures like those in "Auroras" and "The Owl."

"Angel Surrounded by Paysans" is an epitome of the important lessons Stevens learned in writing both *Transport to Summer* and *The Auroras of Autumn*. The countrymen assert the down-to-earth, ignorant-man-again ordinariness of the need for a poetry of the here-and-now which also retains at least the fiction of an absolute or angelic point of view.[4] And as all of *Auroras* seeks to show,

> Yet I am the necessary angel of earth,
> Since, in my sight, you see the earth again,
>
> Cleared of its stiff and stubborn, man-locked set,
> And, in my hearing, you hear its tragic drone
>
> Rise liquidly in liquid lingerings,
> Like watery words awash; . . .

If only momentarily, the congealed imagination of the common man can be made liquid, if the earth is seen again from an absolute point of view, even if that point of view is that of Death. But if Death is "an apparition apparelled in/Apparels of such lightest look that a turn/Of my shoulder and quickly, too quickly, I am gone," then it is essentially as merciful as "she that says good-by" in "The Owl."

II   The Rock

In *The Rock* Death's merciful angel of earth is largely displaced by an image of the old poet as an unborn or sleeping child. The more imminent death seemed to Stevens, the more his imagination meditated on images of rebirth or awakening. "An Old Man Asleep" sets the tone: neatness of plan (the two worlds, the self and the earth, are sleeping); gentle self-irony about that neatness ("your whole peculiar plot"); and the almost foolish running together of external sounds and the snoring of the sleeper ("the drowsy motion of the river R."). "An Old Man Asleep" is a slighter, defter treatment of half the theme in "Questions Are Remarks," the drowsy infantilism of senility.

"The Irish Cliffs of Moher" begins with a question like that of the old man in "Questions Are Remarks," ("Mother, my mother, who are you?") and brings it out of the shadow of irony into plain statement: "This is my father or, maybe,/It is as he was,/A likeness, one of the race of fathers: earth/And sea and air." Senile infantilism is transformed into its vigorous opposite.

"The Plain Sense of Things" accomplishes a similar delicate transformation of tone, from a suggestion of the "fantastic effort" of the earth's imagination, expressed by summer, to the plain sense of things, "silence of a rat come out to see." The necessity of the latter, unlike the possibility of the former, is not attractive. But neither is it repulsive; and, most of all, it is also an effort of the imagination, only not a fantastic one. It is perhaps the noblest one, because it is an effort to choose what has to be. To choose, however, is to take responsibility and to risk guilt. In "One of the Inhabitants of the West," an ideal prophetic poet, given the freedom of "the establishments/Of wind and light and cloud" (the "great structure," the "fantastic effort," in "The Plain Sense of Things"), is able to see and praise the evening star, which sparkles pleasantly on the stony city scene; but he is also free to suppose that the same star is a drop of blood, that the "men of stone" were once flesh and blood, and that they had been turned to stone by looking at the necessitous aspect of earth, at its " 'Horrid figures of Medusa'." One may recall "Blue Guitar" (XVI): "The earth is not earth but a stone,/Not the mother that held men as they fell/But stone"; and one may glance ahead to "Madame la Fleurie": "His grief is that his mother should feed on him, himself and what he saw,/In that distant chamber, a bearded queen, wicked in her dead light." The plainest sense of things may appear to be the freest, most innocent choice of what has to be; but that appearance may conceal one's guilt for having rejected and buried one's mother. Or, the plainest sense of things may be precisely that rejection and that burial. In the first instance one was not free when one made the choice but guilty and compulsive; in the second, one's apparently free act of acceptance was really an act of rejection that damned one eternally. The confident freedom that Stevens felt in *Transport to Summer* (cf. especially "Dutch Graves") has dwindled to the weary wisdom of seeing the balance between freedom and necessity, imagination and reality, mother and father, as an inescapable stalemate.

All one can do with that life-weary wisdom is play around, as the title of the next poem, "Lebensweisheitspielerei," indicates. All one's heroes (such as one's father, as in "The World Without Peculiarity"), as one finally sees them plainly, are "finally human," unaccomplished, indigent. Although now "Each person completely touches us/With what he is and as he is," such touching is only possible "In the stale grandeur of annihilation" and is therefore only a form of playing around. But playing around can be either childish or childlike, and in "The Hermitage at the Center" (which is designed like "The World Without Peculiarity") Stevens chooses the latter alternative. This time it is the mother who is reduced from her summer fullness to "a great thing tottering"; but step by step with her realistic reduction, the imagination focuses in on her *human* eminence until she is seen with "lucent children round her in a ring."

And yet, such a construction, paralleling autumn's destruction of summer, can be barbarous and harshly real, so that there is little to choose between the two, as in "The Green Plant." Indeed, it may be a way in which the hitherto motherly earth, or the deceased earthly mother, rejects the poet, as in "Madame La Fleurie." If "his mother should feed on him, himself and what he saw," in order to send up the glaring green plant, then there is not only no end to guilt, but also the doubling and redoubling of guilt through the endlessness of revenge. "Madame la Fleurie" is the nadir to the zenith of "Dutch Graves."

When life was nothing but ashes in the mouth, Stevens could turn to Santayana, the only poet-philosopher whom he called, in print, "master." "To an Old Philosopher in Rome" gravely and tenderly celebrates the life-wisdom of a man who endured the evil in life "with the politest helplessness" ("Esthetique du Mal," XIII) and yet sustained a sturdy faith in both the common animality of man's life and the uncommon spirituality of which it is capable. At the time this poem was written, Santayana was dying in Rome and was being cared for by nuns. The poem moves up and down between the real and the ideal as if seeking an architectural image that is neither that of the "fantastic effort" that failed in "The Plain Sense of Things," nor the stony city of "One of the Inhabitants of the West," but one which makes "the naked majesty" of Rome the threshold of "the celestial possible." It is in the figure of Santayana himself that this image finally finds its focus: his is the ultimate poverty of "bird-nest arches and of rain-stained-vaults," and it is the celestial as well as the mundane "design of all his words" that "takes form/And frame from thinking and is realized."

In the essay, "Imagination as Value," Stevens says: ". . . it may be assumed that the life of Professor Santayana is a life in which the function of the imagination has had a function similar to its function in any deliberate work of art or letters. We have only to think of this present phase of it, in which, in his old age, he dwells in the head of the world, in the company of devoted women, in their convent, and in the company of familiar saints, whose presence does so much to make any convent an appropriate refuge for a generous and human philosopher" (*NA*, 147-48). In "A Collect of Philosophy," Stevens adds this: "In the case of Santayana, who was an exquisite and memorable poet in the days when he was, also, a young philosopher, the exquisite and memorable way in which he has always said things has given so much delight that we accept what he says as we accept our own civilization. His pages are part of the *douceur de vivre* and do not offer themselves for sensational summary" (*OP*, 187). Stevens believed that Santayana designed his life as he designed his words and was able, therefore, to find for himself and for his readers the *douceur de vivre*, both in life and in death, and possibly to escape the guilty fears (that he had rejected or killed his mother) which Stevens expressed in "One of the Inhabitants of the West" and in "Madame la Fleurie."

"Vacancy in the Park" is one more look at those fears; it appears to be a deliberately humble and meager look, placed as it is right after the celebration of Santayana's poor body and his generous spirit. The image is again architectural, or rather it becomes more and more so, beginning with the absence of an unknown person. The footprints in the snow in the public park at first call up the romantic image of a boat, then a woman's guitar on a table, then a house, then an arbor, and finally "mattresses of vines." The movement is from outdoor to indoor to outdoor scenes, carrying the essence of the indoor scene ("mattresses") back into the outdoor scene. The irrevocable loss of parents ("mattress" suggests both "mater" and "matter") pursues Stevens wherever he goes. He can never achieve the artistic sweetness of life that he believes Santayana achieved.

Nor can Stevens achieve the order, unless the bitter and chaotic sea is "his unique and solitary home," as he concludes in "The Poem that Took the Place of a Mountain." Even the mountain-shaped poem that gives him the natural-artificial mattress on which to lie and look at the sea is a relatively shapeless structure, as his many mountain images usually insist. Stevens felt he could take for his observation post a form (the mountain) that was only slightly less formless than the formless sea (see for instance "This Solitude of Cataracts" in which waves are called "thought-like Monadnocks"). In the context established by "To an Old Philosopher," Stevens may be contrasting his mountain with Santayana's Rome.

"Two Illustrations that the World Is What You Make It" emphasizes the ephemeral character of the order discovered in chaos. It is like one's sense of becoming the wind on an otherwise dirty, withered, winter day; and it is as occasional as "a Sunday's violent idleness" (like "indigence" in "Lebensweisheit-spielerei"). Or, it is like the moment when he becomes "a blue abulge" while looking at a spruce; and afterwards, after this summertime maximum, "his mastery/Left only the fragments found in the grass," "half a shoulder and half a head/To recognize him in after time."

But there is the danger, discovered in "Prologues to What is Possible," that these marble fragments may not recognize him, or that he may not recognize them as comparable with himself. "Prologues" begins with an image of a stone boat bearing the solitary poet to his unique and solitary home—to a central, angelic consciousness that is a condition of absolute poverty and yet one in which he needs no shore, no man, no woman. Although the boat is made of the commonplace stones of his familiar world, those stones shine in such a way that they have lost their heaviness and show their "far-foreign departure" and equally alien destination. While he is in the boat, before it is shattered by its arrival at the imageless center, he is part of its fiery character; but, once he arrives, he does not recognize the self that belongs to the boat. This frightens him.

> By this he knew that likeness of him extended
> Only a little way, and not beyond, unless between himself
> And things beyond resemblance there was this and that
>   intended to be recognized,
> The this and that in the enclosures of hypotheses
> On which men speculated in summer when they were half asleep.

The poem concludes with a long rhetorical question: "what self, for example, did he contain that had not been loosed?"

Although "Looking across the Fields and Watching the Birds Fly" does not answer this question directly, it makes the plausible suggestion that that self may be the spirit which comes from "the body of the world," and, although that spirit may be "a pensive nature, a mechanical/And slightly detestable *operandum*" and "Not one of the masculine myths that we used to make," it is nevertheless "A glass aswarm with things going as far as they can."

One reason for considering this suggestion, even on the edge, rather than at the center, of things, is that the sun uncreates and creates the world in a manner much like that of the mind. So, in "Song of Fixed Accord," the dove in the belly and on the roof accepts the ordinary glares of all the suns: "the sun of five, the sun of six" and so on, each one of them fixed, *for her*; but the sun, *for himself*, makes much "within her." "Song of Fixed Accord" is the most successful of the dove poems. The images latent in the other four ("Depression before Spring," "Thinking of a Relation Between the Images of Metaphor," "The Dove in the Belly," and "The Dove in Spring") are brought to a clear, simple focus.

"The World as Meditation" elevates the dove to Penelope, brings the sun down to Ulysses, and in the process reverses the fears in "Madame la Fleurie" and in "Prologues to What Is Possible." If the poet can never quite reach his unique and solitary home, and if all the treasure he needs to bring there is his empty, yearning arms, then the woman who waits for him there cannot devour him; or, if she does, she devours only his poverty and his need, the very nothingness-of-self of which he is afraid in "Prologues."

What most qualifies Penelope for the role of inverted Madame la Fleurie is the maternal image:

> But was it Ulysses? Or was it only the warmth of the sun
> On her pillow? The thought kept beating in her like her heart.
>
> The two kept beating together.

The poet, who identifies with Ulysses, says to himself at the end of the next poem, "Long and Sluggish Lines": "You were not born yet when the trees were crystal/Nor are you now, in this wakefulness inside a sleep."

The image of the old poet as an unborn or sleeping child appears in several late poems: "The Owl," in which the mythopoetic mind is "A child that sings itself to sleep"; "Questions Are Remarks"; and the later, unpublished expansion of the Ulysses theme, "The Sail of Ulysses," in which the mind's need for myth is again "A child asleep in its own life," a line which became the title of a poem. The image in every case conveys a genuine grandfatherly self-consciousness, but in none so deftly as the one at the end of "Long and Sluggish Lines." It comes at the end of an increasingly whimsical series of images of the conflict between fixed, familiar perceptions and the beginnings of the life of the imagination in new "pre-personae."

The same theme is treated rather more gravely in "A Quiet Normal Life," which is constructed partly on the pattern of "The House Was Quiet" and partly that of "Nomad Exquisite." "A Quiet Normal Life" is not a two-part harmony of the artificial house-self with the natural world-self, as in "The House Was

Quiet," but one of the artificial world-self of his previous poems and the natural house-self of his ever-new-born imagination. The latter is both "the oldest and warmest heart . . . cut/By gallant notions on the part of night" and "his actual candle" which "blazed with artifice."

The same inversion of natural and artificial, house and world, underlies "Final Soliloquy of the Interior Paramour." This time there is not only a candle but a shawl, and the house has become the mother in whose womb the unborn old poet finds that his unique and solitary (it is a soliloquy) home has an order as complete as that of the Christian myth: "Within this vital boundary, in the mind,/We say God and the imagination are one. . . ." All the doubts and fears, from those of "Debris of Life and Mind" to those of "Madame la Fleurie" are finally, if only for a moment, put to rest in this poem.

"The Rock" is Stevens' summary effort to capture the solid-turning-liquid relationship between necessity and freedom, and the success of the poem depends upon an unusual conviction of innocence and freedom, such as that expressed in "Final Soliloquy." "The Rock" begins with an image of childhood "freedom of air" in "the houses of mothers" (cf. the house-womb image in "Final Soliloquy") turned into the rock-like rigidity of the same houses seventy years later. The childhood freedom seems "fantastic." In "The Plain Sense of Things" such a structure as these "houses of mothers" showed itself to be "A fantastic effort" that "has failed." But in "The Rock" the memory of the "fantastic consciousness" of childhood partially liberates the poet from his image of the present rock, elaborating out of its nothingness and its cold desire for illusion the green leaves that come and cover it and bloom into a new birth of sight and life and being.

This leafing-out and this blooming are at first only a partial liberation, for they seem to be evasions, images that separate themselves from reality. In Part II, "The Poem as Icon," Stevens goes higher and deeper, into a fruit-for-the-senses image on the one hand, and a sensuous root for the mind on the other. The present sun on the present rock revives love, which revives the senses, which in turn make the rock swarm with "such imagery/That its barrenness becomes a thousand things/And so exists no more." The idea is the same as that in "A Quiet Normal Life":

when "the oldest and the warmest heart" is cut by the night, its "actual candle" blazes with artifice.

The image of the rock, contrasted with that of the childhood "freedom of air," calls up more plausibly than elsewhere in Stevens' poetry an image of rock-like nothingness (the shadow of Chocorua, and the summer height in "Credences"). The image of rock-like nothingness may be said to be Stevens' most basic image, always latent, never quite manifest, and the most fertile rock bottom of all his fictive constructions. It is the needy, necessitous nature of man, and what makes man most able to replace God as the creative nothingness out of which the world can be reborn.[5] That replacement is the gist of Part III of "The Rock," "Forms of the Rock in a Night-Hymn," and the two poems that follow it: "St. Armorer's Church from the Outside" and "Note on Moonlight." "Note on Moonlight" ends with one of the most succinct statements of the whole idea:

> The one moonlight, the various universe, intended
> So much just to be seen—a purpose, empty
> Perhaps, absurd perhaps, but at least a purpose,
> Certain and ever more fresh. Ah! Certain for sure . . .

As a poet of the air breathed out of a rock-like nothingness, Stevens quite appropriately calls himself "Ariel" at the beginning of "The Planet on the Table." The title of the poem may be taken as the final form of Stevens' metaphor of the natural world within the artificial house. It somewhat belies the conclusion of the poem—that it is not important that his poems survive—for what is the purpose of a house if not to preserve order, to be a place of economy in the midst of "waste and welter"?

But houses fall, and the perpetual flux of things is best represented by a river. "The River of Rivers in Connecticut" is the fertile motion of "presence" ("St. John and the Back-Ache"), the one inexplicable, uncrossable element between the "establishments" ("One of the Inhabitants of the West") of light and air and Stygia, the rock-like nothingness liquified into Death. Like the one moonlight and the various universe in "Note on Moonlight," the purpose of the river is empty: it "flows nowhere, like a sea." And, since it is first simply "this side of Stygia" and then "far this side of Stygia," one is reminded of the ever-approaching but never-arriving Ulysses in "The World as Meditation."

The poet's unique and solitary home is not the Stygian rock but the river-of-rivers-like need for illusion inherent in the rock; between the two is "the difficult inch,/On which the vast arches of space/Repose" in "The Sail of Ulysses" (*OP*, 103). Complete identity of man and thing is death. Only in resemblance, in the difficult inch of difference between man and thing, is there a life.

"And yet" ("Ordinary Evening") that difficult inch is "like/A new knowledge of reality," in the final poem of *The Collected Poems of Wallace Stevens*, which is entitled "Not Ideas about the Thing but the Thing Itself." That is, one looks at the rock, or listens to a bird's "scrawny cry": one *attends* the thing itself. The "first idea" ("Notes") is a simple pointing gesture, like that of the two-year-old in "Questions Are Remarks," who points to the sun and asks, "What is that?"

CHAPTER 5

Conclusion:
The Prose, the Uncollected Poems,
and Stevens' Place in the Traditions

I *The Prose*

IN HIS ESSAY, "A Collect of Philosophy," Stevens indicates that his interest in philosophy is almost entirely an interest in the metaphors that it generates. Furthermore, he modestly suggests that any philosophy's vitality and power to survive depends on its metaphors. He uses as an example "The concept of the infinity of the world," which he believes is "inherently poetic"; that is, it is a concept that continues to excite the imagination of everyone, at least sometimes, whereas Leibnitz's concept of monadic creation is too methodical, too afraid of ornament, and so "looks like a curious machine, several centuries old." Similarly, the idea of the time-lag between sensation and perception transforms the material world into an immaterial one in which, according to Whitehead, "everything is everywhere at all times" (another version of the infinity of the world); but Schopenhauer, like Leibnitz, had to pursue a like transformation in a too methodical, too grotesque, way, objectifying the ultimate will of things step by step, from teeth and throat and bowels to the outer reaches of insensate space.

Although in the course of the essay Stevens withdraws somewhat from the sharpness of this distinction, it remains central: ". . . it is what philosophers find on the way that constitutes the body of philosophy for if the end is appointed in advance neither logic nor the lack of it can affect their passage" (*OP*, 194);

". . . the philosopher's world is intended to be a world, which yet remains to be discovered . . . and the poet's world is intended to be a world, which yet remains to be celebrated" (*OP*, 199). "The confidence of the philosopher might be a certainty with respect to something left behind. The confidence of the poet might be a more immediate certainty" (*OP*, 199). "The philosopher intends his integrations to be fateful; the poet intends his to be effective" (*OP*, 197). Poetry, whether that of poets or of philosophers, is an immediate transformation and celebration of the whole cosmos, as one confidently believes it to exist in the as-yet-unperceived sensations—that is, it is a virtual achievement of God's view of things—whereas philosophy is an exploration of the perceived world, the world left behind by the senses. Stevens concludes that the leaping effectiveness of the poet's integrations is most similar to the philosophy of science. And he uses as an example Planck's speculation that, for the causal bond to be absolute, it would have to be an action of a supra-natural intelligence, or a working hypothesis. Stevens points out that this working assumption is a "willingness to believe beyond belief" that is inherently poetic and characteristically modern.

By the central distinction that he makes in "A Collect of Philosophy" Stevens indicates more clearly than anywhere else why and in what way he was a poet, rather than a philosopher or a writer of prose. Both prose and philosophy demand a step-by-step consecutiveness; and, in trying to see the point of the sequence in which he placed his poems in his books, the reader may have seen again and again that, although occasionally he would follow out the implications of a particular metaphor or theme, more often he would upset it, proclaim its opposite, change his tone from heavy to light or light to heavy. As he says in "A Collect," "the probing of the philosopher is deliberate . . . [but] the probing of the poet is fortuitous." For the philosopher, the thesis is the dog; the example is the tail. And so is it, too, for Stevens, except that the tail wags the dog. For Stevens the example is inevitably a metaphor; and his theory of metaphor is that it accomplishes a change so profound, both in thought and in things, that it is the type of all order in all chaos.

Like "A Collect," the rest of Stevens prose is concerned with his theory of metaphor. "The Noble Rider and the Sound of Words" begins with a brief history of a conventional image of nobility, a man driving or riding a horse; and then the rest of the essay considers the possibilities of imagining nobility in a world in which the primary reality is the blasting force of war. Stevens' general point is that the imagination, and the metaphors it produces, are noble—that is, able to resist the pressure of reality—when they adhere to reality. "The Figure of the Youth as Virile Poet" makes the same point but does so in the context of the difference between the philosopher's and the poet's ways of seeking the truth. The difference in this essay is the same one that he finds in "A Collect."

"Three Academic Pieces," an essay and two poems, proclaims in the title that the theme of imagination adhering to reality has become an academic exercise. The essay begins with a self-mocking statement of his thesis: "The accuracy of accurate letters is an accuracy with respect to the structure of reality." But he seriously adds to his idea an important distinction: metaphor is resemblance, a near likeness that is fertile, because it is above all a relationship, whereas mere identity is sterile, because it is not a relationship. The two poems "Someone Puts a Pineapple Together" and "Of Ideal Time and Choice," illustrate this distinction.

Stevens, in "About One of Marianne Moore's Poems," first finds this distinction between resemblance and identity to be the vital heart of Miss Moore's individual version of reality. Then he illustrates the same vitality in a personal experience of his own: visiting an ancestral graveyard and then seeing an exhibition of illustrated books in the Morgan Library. In "Effects of Analogy" he further analyzes the distinction between resemblance and identity, emphasizing, as in the essay on Moore, the personality of the artist as the decisive differentiating factor. "Imagination as Value" expands this emphasis to include the cultural values of the society in which the poet lives: everything from its search for metaphysical truth to its everyday decorum, but carefully excepting politics and morals. Politics and morals, inasmuch as they impose *external* obligations on the artist, are ruled out because they interfere with the essentially fortuitous character of metaphor.

"The Relations between Poetry and Painting" is an extended analogy between the two arts and an example of how their resemblance fecundates the imagination.

"Two or Three Ideas" can be summarized as follows: "the style of a poem and the poem itself are one"; "the style of the gods and the gods themselves [are] one"; "the style of men and men themselves are one." These are "two or three" ideas because the resemblance between any two of them generates the third. This point is best illustrated in the essay by various translations of the first line of Baudelaire's "La Vie Antérieure": "J'ai long-temps habité sous de vastes portiques": "A long time I lived beneath tremendous porches . . . I lived, for long, under huge porticoes . . . A long time I passed beneath an entrance roof." Each translation emphasizes a different aspect of the two-three-way analogy—the poetic, the theological, or the humanistic—without losing touch with the other two.

"The Irrational Element in Poetry," like "The Effects of Analogy," emphasizes "the transaction between reality and the sensibility of the poet." In doing this, it states the need of the poet to convert the pressure of reality—of war—"into a different, an explicable, an amenable circumstance."

II The Uncollected Poems

In this rapid survey of Stevens' prose, one can see how central metaphor was to Stevens' theory of poetry. One can get an inkling of how important it was in his practice of poetry by looking at his uncollected poems reprinted in *Opus Posthumous*. They are, for the most part, too "rhetorical"—that is, too self-explanatory. This quality is most obviously true of those that were put into books in the 1930's and then left out of *The Collected Poems*: "Owl's Clover," "Life on a Battleship," and "The Woman That Had More Babies Than That." Stevens apparently felt that these three poems were too topical—too much like journalism or even propaganda. But, more fundamentally, they did not sufficiently allow metaphor to create its own metamorphosis. Instead, they guided that metamorphosis in a too methodical, mechanical way. They are like long trains of powder leading to no charges of dynamite; although somewhat illuminating, they have no blasting power.

The neatest example of Stevens' application of his criterion for excluding poems from *The Collected Poems* is provided by the two poems, "The Sail of Ulysses" and "Presence of a External

Master of Knowledge." Both are in *Opus Posthumous*, but "Presence" is there perhaps only because it was written too late to get into *The Collected Poems*. Or, if it wasn't too late, it represents an attempted rescue of a bad poem.

"The Sail of Ulysses" is long, wooden, and thoroughly self-explanatory. No metaphor is allowed to explode; each is carefully disassembled, almost as if to *prevent* its exploding. One can learn a great deal from "The Sail of Ulysses," especially about Stevens' central analogies between need and necessity, and the right to know and the right to be. But, as the poem presents these analogies, they are insistently *identities*; and, as such, they paralyze rather than liberate the reader's perceptions and feelings.

In "Presence of an External Master of Knowledge," a synopsis of "The Sail of Ulysses," Stevens simply juxtaposes the chief metaphors with the chief conclusions. The metaphors are thereby allowed to take over and, in their vigor, to play their own particular havoc with the conclusions. Indeed, true to the metaphor in the title of "The Sail of Ulysses," a conclusion is like a small sail on a large, relentless sea.

III   *The Traditions*

Stevens' place is therefore clearly in the tradition of existentialist romanticism.[1] The fertile fact or sensation is primary; everything, including the existence or non-existence of God, follows from that. The only order worth looking for is the order of chaos itself. Perhaps the writer most akin to him, in this century, is Virginia Woolf; *The Waves*, especially, contains many passages that sound word for word like Stevens. If one looks for the most recent philosophical and literary roots of this attitude, one finds them in the German romanticism of the early nineteenth century, especially in Hegel's dialectic of self-parody and its poetic counterparts in Heine and then in Laforgue.[2] The central principle, again and again in Stevens' poetry, is that no fiction can stand; every fiction must contain the seeds of its own destruction, except the fiction of an absolute.

In America, Stevens' attitude toward poetry and truth is most easily identified with the Emerson-Whitman-William James tradition: the tradition of romantic idealism brought down to an earthy, capricious immediacy.[3] But Stevens is more self-consciously a citizen of the world than any of these men. Apparently his college idol was George Santayana, who was able to smile with genuine sympathy at the stubborn and evil disorder of this world and, at the same time, to delight in the essential order discoverable, especially by the poet, within that disorder. But Stevens' elegance is not like Santayana's; Stevens depends too much on verbal fireworks, "whirroos/And scintillant sizzlings," everything from flicks and flitters to sky-wide booms and deep subterranean or submarine quakings. These explosions are carefully set off by much plain prosaic meditation, the delicate processes of unspoken thought, and periodic didactic announcements. Santayana was a much more subtly masked rider of the heart's barely broken horse. And yet Santayana and Stevens resemble each other so closely[4] that it is no wonder that the analogy between them stimulated Stevens to write one of his finest poems, "To an Old Philosopher in Rome."

Among the essentially international modern poets writing in English—most importantly Pound, Yeats, and Eliot—Stevens occupies an increasingly illuminating position. If one takes Stevens' central problem to be the one expressed in his adagium, "Life is an affair of people not of places. But for me life is an affair of places and that is the trouble," and if one looks then at the other three poets from the point of view of this problem or concern, one sees that, in terms of over-all poetic strategy, Stevens resembles the three of them more than he differs from them. The four poets typically begin with a depersonalized, dehumanized scene and strive to evoke a person from that scene. They then strive to reveal what that person leaves of himself inherent in the scene after he has departed from it. The person evoked tends to be somewhat superhuman, a hero or a saint or even a god, but the direction is nevertheless from place to person and then back to place again.

In Eliot's poetry the reader moves from Prufrock's repression and inanition to Gerontion's empty head-house to the "little life" images at the beginning of *The Waste Land* to the full images of the waste land and the hollow men who inhabit it. All these scenes are more haunted than inhabited. Then, at last, in Part IV of *Ash-Wednesday* the saving lady is evoked; and, when she departs, she leaves her color, her inherently blessing presence, in Part V, "In the last desert between the last blue rocks." Or the evocation in *Little Gidding* of "a familiar compound ghost," who accompanies Eliot on his patrol as an air raid warden, fades with the all clear whistle; but he shows his presence again in the echo of Milton, "The dove descending . . ." transfiguring the hellish scene of modern warfare into an image of grace.

Pound, in his involvement with Oriental literature, found an archetype for this pattern, the Noh drama of Japan. In a Noh play, the initial scene is usually one of little or no life: the famous warrior, Kagekiyo, is a blind old beggar; Genji, an old wood-cutter; Kumasaka, an old priest. Then the action of the play produces an epiphany of the warrior in his former glory, only to undo that action in the end, leaving the scene as it was to begin with, with the difference that now its commonplace features are fraught with the re-enacted glory. Pound seems to have followed the same pattern in *Cantos*. Walking like Dante through the various hells or wastelands, East and West, past and present, with John Adams for a Virgil, Pound evokes his own personality as the type of the poet. He does so by every conceivable device of tone and judgment, but most of all by the unremitting refreshment of his talk. He appears in wondrous clarity to one's ears. But one is forewarned by the first two Cantos that his trajectory is tragic: into Circe's pigsty, into Hades, into beastliness. The *Pisan Cantos* come as a climax to a self-fulfilling prophecy; and Pound pulls down his vanity, accepts the role of an ant, and leaves the withered scene with everything that the quality of his affection for the dreaded mother-mistress (Gea, Aphrodite, Persephone) has carved in his mind. What his affection has carved in his mind is indestructible, perdurable not merely as a possibility but as an actuality in one's way of seeing the scene of the Disciplinary Training Center near Pisa. Down to the tiniest non-human detail, Pound's vibrant voice is there: "When the mind swings by a grass blade/an ant's forefoot shall save you."

Yeats, too, in his most memorable poems moves from the non-human to the human and back. The possibilities made actual in the final scene of a Yeats poem tend to be ghastlier or more glorious than in the poems of Eliot, Pound, and Stevens; but, taken as efforts to be accurate about the potential beastliness or blessedness in the world, the flowing earth in which Pound is both drunk and drowning in Canto 81, or the dove descending in Eliot's *Little Gidding*, or the "rat come out to see" in Stevens' "The Plain Sense of Things"—none of these images is very different in intention from that of the rough beast slouching toward Bethlehem to be born, in Yeats's "Second Coming," or the "rich horn" (ceremony) and the "laurel tree" (custom) in "A Prayer for my Daughter."

Stevens' paradigmatic humanizing-dehumanizing poem is, as one might expect, "Notes Toward a Supreme Fiction," at the end of which the earth-mother stops revolving except in crystal; and the fictive hero becomes the real dead soldier. Even in the one poem written to and about a specific person, "To an Old Philosopher in Rome," the final scene is pure architecture, but architecture that has been filled and made radiant with Santayana's words:

> Total grandeur of a total edifice,
> Chosen by an inquisitor of structures
> For himself. He stops upon this threshold,
> As if the design of all his words takes form
> And frame from thinking and is realized.

Notes and References

Chapter One

1. Paul Rosenfeld, *Men Seen* (New York: Dial Press, 1925), p. 159.
2. George Santayana, *The Sense of Beauty* (New York: Charles Scribner's Sons, 1896), p. 235.
3. Frank Kermode, *Wallace Stevens* (New York: Charles Scribner's Sons, 1960), p. 48.
4. W. R. Keast, "Wallace Stevens' 'Thirteen Ways of Looking at a Blackbird,'" *Chicago Review*, VIII (1954), 48-63.
5. Michel Benamou, "Le Thème du Héros dans la Poésie de Wallace Stevens," *Etudes Anglaises*, XII (1959), 222-30.
6. Clark Griffith, in a lecture at the University of Iowa, summer, 1959.
7. Friedrich Nietzsche, *Ecce Homo*, in *The Philosophy of Nietzsche* (New York: The Modern Library), p. 842.

Chapter Two

1. "Farewell to Florida" begins the 1936 edition of *Ideas of Order*. The deluxe edition of 1935 begins with "Sailing after Lunch." The order in which the poems are placed in the 1936 edition was apparently the one that satisfied Stevens, for he retained it in *The Collected Poems*.
2. "The Idea of Order at Key West" was first published in 1934; "Farewell to Florida," in 1936.
3. In a letter to Renato Poggioli, Stevens says the rabbi in this poem is "a rhetorical rabbi." But he goes on to say, "Frankly, the figure of the rabbi has always been an exceedingly attractive one to me because it is the figure of a man devoted in the extreme to scholarship and at the same time to making some use of it for human purposes." *Mattino Domenicale ed Altre Poesie*, a cura di Renato Poggioli (Torino: Giulio Einaudi; 1953), p. 185.
4. Babette Deutsch, *Poetry in Our Time* (New York: Columbia University Press, 1956), p. 252.
5. Charles Henri Ford, "Verlaine in Hartford," *View*, I, 1 (Sept., 1940), 1, 6.
6. Pablo Picasso, "Conversation avec Picasso," reported by Christian Zervos, in *Cahiers d'Art*, X, 10 (1935), 173-78. A translation of this appears in Alfred Barr, *Picasso* (New York: The Museum of Modern Art, 1946), pp. 272-74.
7. N. P. Stallknecht, "Absence in Reality," *Kenyon Review*, XXI (Fall, 1959), 546.
8. Benamou, p. 226.
9. Crane Brinton *et al.*, *A History of Civilization* (New York: Prentice-Hall, 1955), II, 597.
10. George Santayana, *Interpretations of Poetry and Religion* (New York: Charles Scribner's Sons, 1900), pp. 166-216.

Chapter Three

1. W. B. Yeats, *The Autobiography of William Butler Yeats* (New York: Doubleday Anchor Book, 1958), p. 176.

2. Daniel Fuchs provides additional arguments for this reading, on the basis of a comparison of "Esthetique du Mal" with Baudelaire's *Les Fleurs du Mal,* in *The Comic Spirit of Wallace Stevens* (Durham, N.C., 1963), p. 191.

3. J. V. Cunningham describes this equilibrium in terms of style in "Tradition and Modernity: Wallace Stevens," in Ashley Brown and Robert Haller, *The Achievement of Wallace Stevens* (Philadelphia, 1962), p. 139.

4. For a striking correspondence of a part of this poem with the process of formal religious meditation, see Louis L. Martz, "Wallace Stevens: the World as Meditation," in Marie Borroff, *Wallace Stevens* (Englewood Cliffs, N.J., 1963), pp. 145-46.

5. Benamou, p. 229, makes a good case for seeing this tramp-like figure as Charlie Chaplin.

Chapter Four

1. For a succinct and transparently Hegelian explanation of this maneuver, see J. Hillis Miller, "Wallace Stevens' Poetry of Being," *English Literary History,* XXXI, 1 (March, 1964), 99-101.

2. Henry W. Wells gives this poem its ultimate celebration, for its emotional insights, in his *Introduction to Wallace Stevens* (Bloomington: Indiana University Press, 1964), pp. 170-72.

3. For an unusually pithy assertion of the necessarily religious character of this "reality," see Northrop Frye, "The Realistic Oriole: A Study of Wallace Stevens," in Borroff, *Wallace Stevens,* pp. 173-74.

4. The only satisfactory account of a particular experience that occasioned a particular Stevens poem is Samuel French Morse's—"Angel Surrounded by Paysans," in "The Native Element," in Brown and Haller, pp. 106-8.

5. For a careful treatment of Stevens' sacramental use of the image of the rock, see Ralph J. Mills, Jr., "Wallace Stevens: The Image of the Rock," in Borroff, pp. 106-8.

Chapter Five

1. Despite the lack of biography, there has been a great deal of speculation about "influences." While waiting for more facts, the interested reader may find the best hints in Frank Kermode's remarks on Bergson and Santayana, in *Wallace Stevens* (New York, 1960), pp. 80-83; and in S. F. Morse's essay, "Wallace Stevens, Bergson, Pater," *English Literary History,* XXXI, 1 (March, 1964), 1-34. And now there are the letters.

2. For brief accounts of Hegel's transformation of romantic irony into a philosophical procedure, see Josiah Royce, *The Spirit of Modern Philos-*

ophy (New York: George Braziller, 1955), pp. 177-81, 204-16; Josiah Royce, *Lectures on Modern Idealism* (New Haven: Yale University Press, 1919, 1964), pp. 147-56; and Jacob Loewenberg, "Introduction" to *Hegel Selections* (New York: Charles Scribner's Sons, 1929), pp. xviii-xliii.

3. For a bibliographical sketch of recent work on Stevens' American connections, see Joseph N. Riddel, *English Literary History*, XXXI, 1 (March, 1964), 135.

4. For a beginning bibliography on this resemblance, see Riddel, p. 131.

Selected Bibliography

PRIMARY SOURCES

1. Poems

Harmonium, first edition. New York: Alfred A. Knopf, 1923.
Harmonium, second edition. New York: Alfred A. Knopf, 1931.
Ideas of Order, first edition. New York: The Alcestis Press, 1935.
Ideas of Order, second edition. New York: Alfred A. Knopf, 1936.
Owl's Clover, New York: The Alcestis Press, 1936.
The Man with the Blue Guitar and Other Poems. New York: Alfred A. Knopf, 1937.
Parts of a World. New York: Alfred A. Knopf, 1942.
Notes Toward a Supreme Fiction. Cummington, Massachusetts: The Cummington Press, 1942.
Esthetique du Mal. Cummington, Massachusetts: The Cummington Press, 1945.
Description Without Place. Sewanee, Tennessee: The University Press, 1945.
Transport to Summer. New York: Alfred A. Knopf, 1947.
Three Academic Pieces. Cummington, Massachusetts: The Cummington Press, 1947.
A Primitive like an Orb. New York: The Gotham Book Mart, 1948.
The Auroras of Autumn. New York: Alfred A. Knopf, 1950.
Selected Poems by Wallace Stevens. London: The Fortune Press, 1952.
Selected Poems by Wallace Stevens. London: Faber and Faber, Ltd., 1953.
The Collected Poems of Wallace Stevens. New York: Alfred A. Knopf, 1954.
Opus Posthumous. New York: Alfred A. Knopf, 1957.
Poems by Wallace Stevens. New York: Vintage Books, 1959.

2. Plays

Opus Posthumous. New York: Alfred A. Knopf, 1957.

3. Prose

Three Academic Pieces. Cummington, Massachusetts: The Cummington Press, 1947.
Two or Three Ideas. Hartford, Connecticut: The College English Association, 1951.
The Necessary Angel. New York: Alfred A. Knopf, 1951.
Opus Posthumous. New York: Alfred A. Knopf, 1957.
Letters of Wallace Stevens. Selected and edited by HOLLY STEVENS. New York: Alfred A. Knopf, 1967.

Selected Bibliography

SECONDARY SOURCES

1. Bibliography

MORSE, SAMUEL FRENCH, JACKSON R. BRYER, and JOSEPH N. RIDDEL. *Wallace Stevens Checklist and Bibliography of Stevens Criticism*. Denver: Alan Swallow, 1963.

2. Concordance

WALSH, THOMAS F. *Concordance to the Poetry of Wallace Stevens*. University Park: Pennsylvania State University Press, 1963.

3. Book-length Studies

FUCHS, DANIEL. *The Comic Spirit of Wallace Stevens*. Durham, N.C.: Duke University Press, 1963. Lively insights into the subject announced in the title.

KERMODE, FRANK. *Wallace Stevens*. New York: Grove Press, 1961. The best book, though a brief one, to date.

PACK, ROBERT. *Wallace Stevens*. New Brunswick, N.J.: Rutgers University Press, 1958. A useful treatment of a few central aspects of Stevens' thought and style.

4. Collections of Critical Articles

BORROFF, MARIE. *Wallace Stevens*. Englewood Cliffs, N.J.: Prentice-Hall, 1963.

BROWN, ASHLEY, and ROBERT S. HALLER. *The Achievement of Wallace Stevens*. Philadelphia: J. B. Lippincott, 1962.

5. Valuable Critical Articles

BEACH, JOSEPH WARREN. *Obsessive Images*. Minneapolis: University of Minnesota Press, 1960. These brief remarks (96, 210-12, 338-40) pin down, better than any others, Stevens' double allegiance: to primary-noon reality and to the romantic imagination.

BENAMOU, MICHEL. "Le Thème du Héros dans la Poésie de Wallace Stevens," *Etudes Anglaises*, XII (1959), 222-30. The best treatment of the development of the image of the hero from Stevens' early to his late poetry.

BLACKMUR, R. P. "Examples of Wallace Stevens." *The Double Agent*. New York: Arrow Editions, 1935. (Also in the Brown and Haller collection, pp. 52-80.) The most famous and rewarding early appreciation of Stevens. As Robert Lowell has said, this must be balanced with Winters' criticism.

ELLMAN, RICHARD. "Wallace Stevens' Ice Cream," *Kenyon Review*, XIX (1957), 89-105. The best treatment of the theme of death.

FRYE, NORTHROP. "Realistic Oriole," *Hudson Review*, X (Fall, 1957), 353-70, and in the Borroff collection, pp. 161-76. A necessary balance to Beach's remarks: Frye finds the center of Stevens' divided loyalties, and makes a good case for a classical synthesis of reason and emotion.

LOWELL, ROBERT. "Imagination and Reality," *The Nation*, CLXVI (April 5, 1947), 400-2. A brief review of *Transport to Summer*; philosophically more penetrating than anything else written about Stevens.

PEARCE, ROY HARVEY. "The Poet as Person," *The Yale Review*, XLI (March, 1952). (Also in Charles Feidelson and Paul Brodtkorb, *Interpretations of American Literature* [New York: Oxford University Press, 1959], pp. 369-86). The classic statement of the difference between Stevens and Eliot.

SCHWARTZ, DELMORE. "The Ultimate Plato with Picasso's Guitar," *The Harvard Advocate* (December, 1940), 11-16. An excellent insight into the continuity of Stevens' subject matter, from the early through the middle period.

WINTERS, YVOR. "The Hedonist's Progress," *In Defense of Reason*. New York: Swallow Press and William Morrow, 1947.

————. *On Modern Poets*. Cleveland: World, 1959. The most famous and useful early attack on Stevens' fundamental attitude toward the world. Must be balanced with Blackmur's appreciation.

Index

This is an index of poems because the plays and the essays can easily be found through the table of contents, and the names of critics, poets, and philosophers are mentioned with the sole purpose of explicating the poems.

Index